I SAW FOR MYSELF

I SAW FOR MYSELF

The Aftermath of Suez

by

ANTHONY NUTTING

Minister of State for Foreign Affairs, 1954-56

DOUBLEDAY & COMPANY INC.

GARDEN CITY N.Y.

1958

CONTENTS

INTRODUCTION

In the following pages I have set down the impressions I gathered early in 1957 from a tour of North Africa and the Middle East. These impressions appeared first of all in a condensed form in the *New York Herald Tribune*. They were also syndicated in newspapers in the United States, the United Kingdom and many other countries.

At the time when these newspaper articles were appearing I had little if any intention of reproducing my conclusions in book form. For one thing I felt that in a short time they would be overtaken by events. For another, having published books but not written any hitherto, I felt a natural hesitation in inflicting myself upon the reading public. But as several people of judgement have pointed out, far from being out of date, my impressions are as valid today as on the day that they were formed. As to the modesty angle, I must admit that my enthusiasm for my conclusions has triumphed over my hesitation to reproduce them again.

The idea of doing a tour of the Middle East was, curiously enough, first put into my head by no less a person than Sir Winston Churchill. It was in 1953, when with Sir Anthony Eden away ill and Mr Selwyn Lloyd in New York, I had been called over to discuss some Middle East problem at No. 10 Downing Street. Sir Winston was firing questions at me with machine-gun rapidity and I was fumbling the answers badly. Eventually, after I had been forced to plead ignorance in reply to some five questions in a row, the Prime Minister looked at me over the top of his glasses and, with that puckish grin so well known to the many victims of his wit in the House of Commons, he said, "But, young man, you are atrociously ill-informed; you must go and visit these parts and see these people and then you can come and see me."

Needless to say, I was all for it. But, with the Foreign Secretary ill, there was a world of difference between the Prime Ministerial injunction and the Prime Ministerial permission to leave the country. As things turned out, such were my preoccupations with Parliament and later with the United Nations that the

nearest I ever got, as a Minister, to visiting the Middle East
was when I went to Cairo in September, 1954 to negotiate the
Anglo-Egyptian Agreement with Gamal Abdul Nasser.

I therefore put aside any thought of Sir Winston's suggested
tour until the end of 1956 when I resigned from the Government in disagreement with the policy of Anglo-French intervention at Suez. Then the idea occurred to me that, having
done what I had done and disassociated myself from an act
which in Arab eyes was a criminal assault upon the whole Arab
world, it was my duty to go to the Middle East and to do whatever was possible to put things right between my country and
our Arab friends. I was strongly urged to do this by friends of
mine in Parliament, especially in my own Party, and in other
official and unofficial walks of life.

After a few weeks spent collecting visas and planning my
itinerary I took off for Morocco on the first stage of a journey
that was to take me over 20,000 miles of the most disturbed
and disturbing area of the modern world. By the time I had
finished I had visited eighteen Middle-Eastern countries and
talked with politicians and peasants, diplomats and students,
oil-men and tribal chieftains. I had discussed the perplexities of
our troubled world personally with King Faisal of Iraq and
King Hussein of Jordan, with King Saud, President Nasser and
Premier Nehru, Nuri-es-Said of Iraq, with Ben Gurion of
Israel, President Camille Chamoun of Lebanon, Iskander
Mirza of Pakistan, Premier Menderes of Turkey, the Rulers of
Kuwait and Bahrain, Premier Habib Bourguiba of Tunisia,
Ben Halim of Libya, Si Bekkai of Morocco and Al Assali of
Syria. Sympathy with the problems and aspirations of these
men and their people was the simple magic key to every door.

Having myself gained from my long journey some understanding of the true feelings and the underlying beliefs of the
Moslem world, I want to pass this on to all who study these
matters with an open, unprejudiced mind. In America and in
Britain there has been too much misunderstanding and con-
fusion about the Middle East and its problems. My hope in the
succeeding chapters is to be able to set things in a true perspec-
tive and to create a better understanding of what the people of
this part of the world seek to achieve, and of how we of the
West can develop a real and honourable partnership with them.

Chapter I

MOROCCO AND TUNISIA

FLYING across Spain to Morocco in the early spring is a surprising experience. I could hardly believe at first that we were not flying away from, instead of towards, Africa. The great central plateau of Spain, emerging from the harsh grip of winter, looked like the Sahara, a barren wilderness of stony ground unrelieved by the villages sleeping beneath a camouflage of grey dust which seems to have settled on them centuries ago never to be swept away. Even the rivers, tracing muddy-brown streaks across the landscape, appear tired and listless, as if they had no longer life to offer to the earth.

By contrast, Morocco wore a European look, the houses freshly painted red and white and blue, the landscape reaching richly green and brown to golden beaches and the broad white rollers of the Atlantic surf. Rabat, the capital of this newly independent State, might be Nice or Cannes. The old Arab town has almost entirely disappeared, giving way to dazzling white stone houses with green gardens and purple bougainvillea. Only the Sultan's palace with the vast maidan square alongside its walls wears the oriental look. But even the palace, with its blue and white tiling over the Moorish arches, might have been built for a motion-picture set rather than for the residence of an Arab monarch.

Could it be, I thought, that this country was as westward looking as it seemed on the surface? After all the bitterness of their struggle for independence it seemed that Morocco and her sister State Tunisia must, at least for the present, be going through a period of anti-Western and anti-European reaction. Only four years ago the French, in a last desperate throw to postpone the coming of Moroccan independence, had deposed the Sultan and sent him in exile to Corsica. In Tunisia they had kept Habib Bourguiba in prison and exile for several years in a parallel effort to maintain French rule. In Algeria, the French were still bitterly holding on against the nationalist tide.

How, then, having won their independence against this same policy of repression, could the Moroccans and Tunisians be prepared to let bygones be bygones and work an amicable political relationship with those who had so recently been an occupation force?

It seemed impossible. Yet it is happening. True there are incidents from time to time. There are still several highly dangerous and delicate issues to be resolved between the Moroccans and Tunisians and the French. But from all that I saw and heard in Morocco and later in Tunisia when I went there to see M. Bourguiba, there is no doubt that these two new Arab States look westwards for friends and partners.

There is about the leaders of these countries none of the neutralism which has infected so many newly independent States. They are not attracted by Nehru's approach to international life. They want to create a North African Federation in close alliance with the West. They want no truck with Soviet Russia. They do not even intend to have diplomatic relations with the Soviets until they have sorted out their relationship with the West.

To the Sultan and his people, and to M. Bourguiba and his, Communism is an evil alien doctrine, contrary in every way to the teachings of the Koran, something too dangerous to permit of any compromise. That is one good reason why neither of them has any use for President Gamal Abdul Nasser, whom they regard as being far too deeply committed to his Russian friends to withdraw from the trap. M. Bourguiba was especially forthright to me in his condemnation of what he called "that apprentice dictator", who had sold out his country to the enemy of all true Arabs and whose subversive meddling in the affairs of his brother Arabs in Tunisia had included a fat subsidy to Salah Ben Youssef, who is now in exile in Egypt and who was the leader of the extreme Tunisian nationalists and quite a thorn in M. Bourguiba's flesh.

Among all the people I spoke to in Morocco, nobody made the position of his country clearer than the Prime Minister, Si Bekkai. Tall and very distinguished, he looks every inch the former infantry colonel in the French army, an impression which is heightened by a pronounced limp, the result of losing a leg while leading his regiment at the Salerno landing during the last war. Speaking with a frankness and forthrightness altogether untypical of the ordinary Arab politician, this engaging product of Arab origins and French culture made it plain to me where his Sultan, his Government and he himself stood. Morocco, he said, did not want to join the Arab league and get involved in all the jealousies, squabbles and intrigues of the Middle East. When I asked what Morocco would join and whether she had contemplated an association with NATO, he did not reject the idea. On the contrary, he seemed interested and attracted by it. He reminded me that the Sultan had spoken of Morocco as a bridge between Africa and Europe and he agreed that with American bases on Moroccan soil there were very definite similarities between Morocco and Turkey as the bridge between Asia and Europe. Si Bekkai was not slow to see that in the days of long-range missiles, Morocco would be very much in the front line of any major war and therefore had a right to be enrolled and treated as a partner in the Western Alliance. (I am bound to confess that in my own judgement Morocco has every bit as much right to membership of NATO as Iceland, if not rather more.)

There is another good reason for Morocco, and Tunisia too, to work out some association with NATO. It would I am sure help to solve the problem of French forces in these two countries. Although France has handed over the reins of government to Moroccan and Tunisian administration, the French—or at least the French military—still behave as if they owned the place. In Morocco there are about 100,000 French troops; in Tunisia about 20,000, plus a vast French naval and air base at Bizerta. They come and go at will and, if any questions are asked or protests lodged at their arbitrary behaviour, the French military are quick to assert their legal right to move forces into and around either country without asking anyone's permission. General Cogny, the officer commanding French forces in Morocco, has been especially tactless in reminding the Moroccan Government that they have no rights even to regulate the number or locations of his troops.

It is true that when the hand-over of power took place no arrangements were made about French forces. Therefore while they have no juridical status—no status of forces agreement such as exists in Europe for NATO forces and bases—there is equally no instrument by which the Moroccan or Tunisian authorities can exercise any control over the numbers or the movements of these French troops.

Si Bekkai and Bourguiba have repeatedly asked the French to work out with them an agreement setting some limitation on numbers and requiring some concentration in properly defined areas, such as Bizerta in the case of Tunisia. But the French retort that they must have uninhibited freedom of movement for their forces, in order to protect the local French populations, to keep guard on the Algerian borders and to prevent smuggling of arms to the Algerian nationalists.

The French studiously ignore that the only real danger to their countrymen in Morocco and Tunisia arises very largely from the behaviour of French forces in those countries and the indignation which this stirs up. As to the Algerian border, Bourguiba pointed out to me with some heat that if the French wanted to guard the frontier from Algeria that is their affair, but he and his countrymen would not tolerate Tunisia being turned into a military base for French attacks upon their Arab brethren in Algeria.

Bourguiba is well within his rights. Besides, this kind of French attitude and action merely plays into the hands of the extreme nationalists. It only helps men like Allal el Fassi, the extreme Istiqlal leader in Morocco, who against the wishes of the Sultan has been stirring up trouble for the French in their neighbouring colony of Mauretania, and who would dearly like to see all French influence removed from Morocco and the whole of French Africa. It also gives a handle to Cairo Radio sneeringly to portray Bourguiba's and the Sultan's Governments as semi-protectorates still under French armies of occupation.

If Morocco and Tunisia were to join in some association with NATO the problem of the French garrisons could be resolved within this framework. These forces would then be stationed on Moroccan and Tunisian territory as NATO forces, their bases would be NATO bases, their numbers and movements would be regulated by agreement with the Moroccan and Tunisian Governments, and their disposition would be subject to some degree of control by NATO in which the voice of Morocco and Tunisia could make itself heard. A solution could then be reached which would take the sting out of Cairo Radio's attacks and yet provide the French with the bases they need.

Nothing could be more in France's interests than to arrive at some such arrangement. Let there be no mistake, Bourguiba, the Sultan of Morocco and Si Bekkai, for all the humiliations they have suffered at French hands, are the best friends that France could have today in North Africa. "I could not have fought the French for so long, had I not loved France so much," was Bourguiba's typically incisive description of his feelings for the country that had given him his culture and the language that he speaks more perfectly than most henchmen.

My talks with the Moroccans and Tunisians left me in no doubt that the Sultan and Bourguiba are anxious to use their influence with the Arabs of North Africa and to counter that of President Nasser and his propagandists. Of course there is some inevitable rivalry between the leaders of these two newly emergent nations. Yet, however they might differ over who would be the boss of any North African Federation, they are at one in resisting and seeking to supplant Egyptian influences in the Arab world. What they need most is help from the West, help in the way of actions as well as words. As Si Bekkai put it to me, "You of the West must help us by showing that the Arabs can be your friends and allies and still be free. You must get over your shyness and reluctance to rub this into the French. You must stop doing things which make the Arabs think that the Russians and Nasser are their only champions."

Clearly Suez and all that was very much in his mind when he said this. But it was not the only thing. As the President of the Moroccan National Assembly and leading newspaper editors bitterly complained to me, France was using strong arm pressure tactics in financial negotiations with Morocco. The country needs French capital investment to arrest growing unemployment. But the French are stalling in the hope that the Moroccans will not press their demands for a status of forces agreement.

As a result, men in high places, like M. Balafrej, Morocco's Foreign Minister, and the Secretary-General of the Istiqlal party, nurse the deepest suspicions of everything the French do. They suspect that France seeks to depose the Sultan once again and to replace him with one of the sons of the late leader of the Berber tribesmen, El Glaoui, whom she supported in the days of the protectorate on the old "divide-and-rule" principle in his opposition to the Sultan, until she was forced to admit that it was the Sultan who commanded the support of the majority of his people. These suspicions are fed by the constant carping resentment which the French show towards Mohammed V and all his works, and to Bourguiba and his.

It is true that the Sultan's writ does not run throughout all Morocco. He has not so far sought to impose his personality upon some of the remoter parts, such as Marrakesh where the Berber tradition is still strong. But, in the rest of the country, his position is being consolidated and quiet reigns where formerly there was much tribal strife. This should continue unless some unavoidable factor intervenes, such as famine, which might drive the hill-tribesmen to pillage in the plains.

As for Bourguiba, his position in Tunisia seems unassailable now that Salah Ben Youssef has been forced to retire to Cairo. His methods are not perhaps as democratic as those of the French National Assembly. His treatment of the ageing Bey of Tunis may have left much to be desired. But no man is more anxious to see, not only Tunisia, but all North Africa enjoying with France that kind of relationship which exists today in the Commonwealth, for which Bourguiba expressed to me an unbounded admiration. Alas, the failure of France to work out such a relationship creates even among some moderate and reasonable Moroccans and Tunisians a fear that France's real purpose, if she can destroy the Algerian nationalists, is to reimpose her rule throughout the whole of North Africa. There is some suspicion that the Eurafrica economic project is the economic corollary of this imperialist design. What folly, therefore, as Si Bekkai told me, that the French failed to consult either the Moroccan or the Tunisian Government before launching a project which is of direct concern to both these countries as African States and as members of the Franc zone.

It is nothing short of a tragedy that France, largely through her own mistakes, should be so suspected in North Africa. France has done much for Morocco and Tunisia but she gets no thanks for it. She has brought them a culture and a prosperity which they could never have acquired for themselves. French officials still help to run the administrations. In Morocco there are still some 40,000 Frenchmen staffing Government posts at every level from Commandant of the Sultan's bodyguard down to Customs Inspectors and postmen. In Tunisia there are fewer French officials, because Bourguiba and his team of enthusiastic young Ministers have done an intensive job of "Tunisification" in building up a new State on the model of Kemal Ataturk's Turkey. But French culture has gone deep and nobody portrays this more than M. Bourguiba himself.

Looking to the future, there is so much that France, Morocco and Tunisia could do for one another if only a real partnership could be worked out. But to do this, the French must accept Moroccan and Tunisian independence with a good grace and show themselves willing to help and not to humiliate their two former protectorates. More than that, they must also make a settlement in Algeria. This is to North Africa what Palestine is to the Middle East. It is a constant poison, a running sore in Franco-Arab relations from Casablanca to Cape Bon. The fiery-eyed look on Bourguiba's face when he spoke of Algeria left me in no doubt that Tunisia and her sister-State Morocco could not offer the French or the West the full co-operation they would like "so long as France persists in a war of extermination against our fellow Arabs". Si Bekkai's only reservation about joining up with NATO was his concern lest this might be taken as condoning French policy in Algeria.

In an hour-long monologue conducted from his bed, where he was resting from his visit to the Ghana independence celebrations, Bourguiba told me of his hopes and fears about the Algerian situation. With many gestures, looking like some minor prophet, drawing diagrams on the eiderdown to illustrate his argument, he affirmed that a solution must and could be found. But if it were not found soon he could not answer for the consequences upon relations between North Africa and the West. Neutralist, Egyptian, maybe even Communist, influences might take over. He was trying his best to prevent this by replacing Egypt as the best friend of the Algerian nationalists. He had tried to persuade them to compromise, to adopt as he did in Tunisia the "foot-in-the-door" tactics. But the French had not helped. "The French are peasants," he said, "they hold on to their land with grim determination, whereas you British are merchants who seek not territory but markets." There is too much truth in this, as I discovered in Algeria itself.

CHAPTER II

ALGERIA

FROM all that I saw in Algeria, I am convinced that if France continues her present policy she will lose Algeria completely. I am equally certain that, if the French Government were to pluck up their courage and pocket a little of their pride, a settlement could be reached, which would secure essential French interests.

But time is not on France's side. The National Assembly in Paris cannot persist any longer in the attitudes of dither and negation which have toppled out one Government because it wanted more money to make war and its successor because it wanted approval to make peace. The National Assembly had better get busy, and quickly, to realize that only with a settlement can French influence in Algeria be saved from extinction at the hands of the extreme nationalists. Every day that passes, every shot that is fired and every killing that takes place in this tragic country only widens the gulf between Frenchman and Arab, only makes it harder for both sides to come together. As Paris becomes more obdurate, the extreme nationalists become more powerful and successful in terrorizing the masses of ordinary Algerians who are inevitably the principal sufferers from this war of attrition.

It is sometimes said that what prevents a settlement is the lack of what the French call *interlocuteurs valables* on the Algerian side. This is barely a half-truth. It could as easily be said that the lack of staying power of almost every French Government prevents the nationalists getting down to negotiations with Paris.

What is really preventing a settlement is that no Frenchman of sufficient standing will contemplate anything which does not keep Algeria tied to France as part of the metropolitan territory, and no Algerian nationalist will accept anything short of independence. If Paris willed it, a compromise could undoubtedly be found between these two points-of-view. If Paris willed it,

the Sultan of Morocco and M. Bourguiba would certainly use
all their influence to bring the nationalists to accept a reasonable settlement. But when the Sultan was trying to bring his
influence to bear in the direction of a settlement upon Ben
Bella, the Nationalist leader, and some of his colleagues, Paris's
contribution to the effort was to kidnap the lot after forcing the
Sultan's aeroplane, in which they were flying and for which
the French Government in Algiers had issued a safe-conduct, to
land in Algerian territory. Small wonder the Sultan should
feel the victim of a piece of double-crossing which gave the lie
to the repeated assertions of the French Ambassador in Rabat
that France was anxiously seeking a settlement.

So far the utmost that Paris has offered towards a settlement
has been, first, elections under international supervision (proposed by M. Guy Mollet) and, more recently, a draft law to
turn Algeria into a federal State (proposed by M. Bourges
Manoury). But, like every other proposal from the French side,
there is not the remotest glimmer of independence in either of
these offers. On the contrary, the elections which M. Guy
Mollet's Government offered early in 1957 were for Algerian
representation in the Paris Assembly, not in an Algerian Parliament in Algiers. This is hardly likely to commend itself to the
F.L.N. (the National Liberation Front). For one thing, the
representation of Algeria in the Paris Assembly up to now has
been a travesty of the French Government's own oft-repeated
assertion that Algeria is a department of France. In France
there is one Deputy for every eighty-thousand inhabitants; in
Algeria there is one for every half-million.

The Bourges Manoury draft law proclaimed that Algeria
should be "composed of federated territories which democratically and freely manage their own affairs". Any hopes that this
high-sounding proclamation might herald the grant of independence were at once dashed by the statement that the
federation of Algeria will remain "an integral part of the French
Republic". Both at the federal and at the territorial level it
was clearly laid down that the French and not the Algerians
should be in charge. There was to be a legislative assembly and
a government in each territory, but the local representative of
the French Republic was to choose the government. After a
lapse of two years there was to be a federal assembly and

government; but the French Republic was to reserve control, not only over foreign relations and defence, but also over the police, security, election procedures, the organization of Algerian political parties, currency, finance, customs, taxes, State expenditure, justice and education.

So the Algerians were to be allowed "democratically and freely to manage their own affairs"!

The post of Governor-General was to be abolished but his powers were to remain and be vested in a French Minister-Resident. It was he and his lieutenant in each territory who would control the Civil Service and have authority over government servants in Algeria—not the Algerian federal or territorial governments. Moreover, just to make quite sure that effectively nothing was changed, the powers of the Minister-Resident and his representatives were to include that of seeing that "the provisions of the present law and of the French Constitution are obeyed".

How any self-respecting nationalist could be expected to accept this mockery of democracy, I fail to see. Yet even this piece of sham was enough for the right-wing parties in Paris to raise the cry of a sell-out and to overthrow the Government which proposed it. The very minimum which the F.L.N. could be brought to accept—and then only with the utmost effort and pressure from their French and Tunisian friends—would be elections for an Algerian Assembly and negotiations thereafter between France and representatives of the Assembly to set a term for the achievement of independence. Breaking the country up into six federated territories, each of which would still be run by French administrators and overlords, smacks too much of the old divide-and-rule policy which France has so often sought to perpetrate in her overseas domains. This point was well taken by M. Bourguiba in his comments when the new *loi cadre* was announced, comments which constituted by far the harshest criticism of French policy that this critic has yet made.

Of course to get discussions going for a cease-fire on any terms would require the release of the Algerian political leaders, including Ben Bella, whom the French have under lock and key. This is not a question of prestige but of practical politics. The present leaders in the field in Algeria are no more than the Maquis-type resistance leaders and would be neither competent nor representative enough to negotiate upon political questions. The political leaders still at large in the country, such as Ferhat Abbas or Krim Belkassem, the leader of the Kabyles on the F.L.N. executive, are not of the required stature. But M. Lacoste obdurately refuses to have Ben Bella and his colleagues released—and Paris supports the Governor-General of Algeria to the hilt.

M. Lacoste, of course, does not want a settlement. For one thing it would lose him his job, and there are few who have been reared among the vicissitudes of French politics who would give up a Government post before it gave them up. But the real reason for French obduracy is not M. Lacoste's determination to stay put himself. It is, as the Secretary-General of the Algerian Government made no attempt to conceal from me, a matter of sheer economic interest. There are prodigious French investments in Algeria which Paris fears would be sequestrated if the nationalists got the power to lay hands on them. Even more important than this is the recent oil strike in the Algerian Sahara.

The French see two heaven-sent prospects in this vitally important discovery. First, they believe that the oil will pay for the war in Algeria, and second, so great is the strike, that they fancy they will soon be independent of Middle East oil and all its problems. I was even told in Algiers that the estimated oil production from these new fields will suffice to meet the oil needs of all Western Europe, less Great Britain. What I did not find in Algiers was any recognition that independence, if it came as the product of a negotiated settlement and not as the outcome of a French defeat, need in no way affect France's oil stake in the Sahara but would enable France to spend the oil revenues on more profitable enterprises than shooting Algerians.

Compared with the hard practical considerations of this new discovery, the oft-repeated emotional argument that any weakening in Algeria would provoke the French residents (*Colons*, as they are called locally) to violent measures, now comes a very poor second. It was never a very valid argument. It is true that when M. Mollet visited Algiers in February, 1956 he was pelted with tomatoes by angry *colons* who feared that his Government was going to abandon them. But there is a large gap between throwing tomatoes at a French Prime Minister and fighting to the death against a hand-over of power to the Algerians who outnumber the Europeans by nine to one.

In any case the numbers of genuine French nationals in Algeria has been greatly exaggerated in the past to support the case that Algeria must remain a department of France. The official estimate is around one and a half million. From all that I could ascertain, the true figure is nearer 500,000. The rest are a mixture of Spanish, Italian, Greek, Levantine and other nationalities. In Oran the European population is overwhelmingly Spanish, the French being the minority. Only in Algiers itself can the French be truly said to predominate.

Besides, it is highly debatable who exactly among the local French would stay to fight it out against the Algerians once the French Government had decided to call it a day. All the well-to-do settlers have taken the precaution of salting money away outside Algeria. Many have large investments in South America. Now a new idea is catching on. It is that there are parts of France as undeveloped as Algeria. The French landlord of a leading foreign Consul-General in Algiers has moved back to France where he has bought himself a number of derelict farms in the Dordogne district, which he estimates will make him a milliard francs ($2¼ million) over the next twenty years.

The Government in Algiers may plaster the walls with posters proclaiming "*L'Algerie Vivra Française*". But, whilst every Frenchman is reinsuring against the day when Algeria becomes Algerian, no amount of posters or slogans will carry conviction or impress in any way upon the local population that France intends to stay put. The plain fact is that the nationalists are convinced that the French are on the way out. The Algiers Government blame this on the few outspoken critics of French policy, such as M. Pierre Mendes France, who was principally responsible for the hand-over of power in Morocco and Tunisia. But, notwithstanding whatever influence M. Mendes France may have on nationalist opinion, the real fault lies with Paris, with the Algiers Government and with the local French, none of whom do anything effective to counter the widespread impression that they will in the end abandon the struggle. The Paris Assembly supports the policy of military action against the nationalists but refuses to vote the money to pay for it.

Hence M. Mollet's fall last May. In Algeria nothing is done to put the French case across to the Arab population. It is not unfair to say that the principal point of contact between the French administration and the nine million Moslems is the bayonet. When I was in Algeria there was not a single French newspaper printed in Arabic throughout the whole of this vast territory. What is more, out of an occupation force numbering half a million men, only 130 speak Arabic. When I drew attention to this, M. Chaussade, the affable Secretary-General of the Algiers Government, and No. 2 to M. Lacoste, shrugged it off with the astonishing assertion that the majority of the Arabs spoke, read and fully understood French. You just cannot argue with that kind of approach.

Nor can you argue with those French in Algeria who still assert that the rebels are only a handful of barbarous bandits. In fact, as a few members of the Algiers Government now admit in whispers, an increasing number of respectable middle-class citizens are supporting the nationalist cause, some by money contributions, others by more active means. Much of this new strength to the F.L.N. probably springs from a desire to reinsure with the nationalists against the day when they and no longer the French are in power. Another factor which is contributing recruits to the National Liberation Front is unemployment, due to over-population and under-investment. (The population increase is at the rate of half a million a year on a present total of a little over ten millions.) Unemployment has hit particularly the youth of the country who, partly in search for adventure and partly for something to do, are joining the F.L.N. in increasing numbers. It is therefore no good blinding oneself to the fact that the nationalist movement is spreading among all sections of the community.

Against this, the French insist that the military situation is much improved compared with a year ago. So indeed it should be with more than half of France's army engaged. The nationalists are suffering heavy casualties and, by the use of some pretty rough methods of investigation upon their captives, the military authorities have been able to find and arrest several minor nationalist leaders. The morale of the French forces, which fell to zero after the rout in Indo-China, has recovered itself, due in no small way to the efforts and personality of its commander, a young rough-diamond paratrooper with a fine record of courage and initiative, General Jacques Massu.

But military measures alone will never defeat the nationalists. This was almost the first thing that M. Chevallier, the Mayor of Algiers, said to me when we met to discuss the Algerian situation. Unhappily the liberal views and reasoned opposition to French policy of this devoted son of France and Algeria are but a faint cry in the wilderness of muddled thinking and false pride which infect his compatriots. "With half a million troops we might one day impose a military defeat on the rebels," he said. "But what will happen when we withdraw the bulk of these forces? The whole trouble will start up again." Besides, as M. Chevallier added, how long will it take to impose the military defeat? Every week one reads of some twenty, thirty or forty Algerians being killed by French forces, but, as fast as they are killed, others take their place.

There is another thing that will keep the struggle going on the nationalist side. The extortion of "protection money" has become a highly profitable racket and gives to too many of its beneficiaries a vested interest in maintaining a state of conflict. Nor is protection money the only aid which the F.L.N. can get without much difficulty. Aid from abroad comes regularly, especially from Tunisia. M. Bourguiba virtually admitted to me that he was lending a lot more than moral support to the Algerian nationalists, and the French certainly have convincing proof of much material help going across the Tunisian border. Yet there is little doubt in my mind—and still less in M. Bourguiba's—that, if help is not forthcoming from Tunisia, Colonel Nasser will step in in a big way. That would mean Russian arms for the F.L.N. and before long the inevitable offer of technicians and so on. The thin end of the most dangerous divisive wedge in the world of today would be driven in and it would then be too late for M. Bourguiba and our other westward-looking friends in North Africa to draw it out. The choice for Tunisia is one of evils, either to hinder the French or to help Nasser and Russia to extend their influence. I am certain that in a difficult situation they have made the only possible choice.

Not unnaturally, Tunisian aid for the F.L.N. infuriates the French, who take the strict view that M. Bourguiba should not interfere outside his own country in matters which are France's affair. Such is the nature of the terrain and the length of the frontier that the French cannot stop this aid getting through without bringing in even more troops to seal off the border. Even if more troops could be found it is highly doubtful whether the French Parliament would vote the extra money. The Algerian emergency is now costing France between one billion and one and a half billion dollars a year. Faced with a roaring economic crisis France cannot afford to go on spending at this rate, still less to increase it. If she will not make peace, she will have to make economies.

It was no doubt with this poor prospect in view that the French authorities early in 1957 abandoned the policy of going all out to beat the F.L.N. into accepting a general cease-fire. Since then they have been pinning their hopes and directing their policy towards pacifying limited areas and achieving local cease-fires. The object is now to hold elections in the "pacified" municipalities and to encourage Moslems to stand for election as mayors and lesser municipal officers. My talks with Moslem leaders convinced me beyond any doubt that such hopes are utterly vain. The revolution has spread too far among the people. Violence has become too prevalent and too powerful a weapon. The terror of being sought out and murdered by the rebel extremists would frighten all but the barest handful of Algerians into refusing to accept any office under French rule, let alone to present themselves as eager and willing candidates. The fear of these bloody reprisals brings a constant stream of resignations by Moslem mayors and sub-prefects. To reverse the stream the French must remove the fear, and that they cannot do without "pacifying" the whole country.

So Algeria remains a tragic deadlock, as it must remain while intransigeance and unreason continue to blind both sides in the struggle. France may today be winning a few battles, but she will not, she cannot, win the war. The Algerian people will never admit the fantastic proposition that they and their land are a part of France. On either side of them they have the example of Morocco and Tunisia—independent States which won their independence after much bloodshed and conflict. Even in Black Africa they know that a far greater degree of autonomy has been granted to the local population than they have ever known in Algeria. With this knowledge of what can be won by keeping up the pressure and keeping on with the fight, the Algerian people will never rest until they too have won their independence.

You feel this clearly as you walk about the towns and villages. You can almost sense it from the deserted streets and darkened houses after the curfew hour has struck. The midnight air is tense with a foreboding silence. Behind the shuttered windows lurks an ominous conspiracy. The rebels have retired to fight another day. In the morning, as Arabs go their way to work along the barricaded streets, the look of hatred, black unrelenting hatred, deepens visibly as they pass one of the hundreds of paratroop patrols who parade the towns by day and night. Behind the sullen, furtive faces burns the passionate flame of nationalism. When you see this, you know that nothing will daunt these people, neither prison, nor torture, nor death. They are dedicated and determined to see the thing through to the end—the end of foreign rule and occupation.

The most dangerous and short-sighted aspect of all French thinking about Algeria is the ignorance, whether real or affected, which so many French politicians show about the true nature and attitude of the Algerian Nationalist movement. "Know your enemy" is a wise adage, but one which Frenchmen seem to have cast aside. In my talk with General Massu he affected what I thought to be a dangerous contempt for the rebels. You can point out that the F.L.N. will have no truck with the Communists, that they have in fact expelled or executed members of their movement who were found to be sympathetic to Communism, and that they have spurned offers of aid from Communist sources. This is only seized upon as proof that the nationalists must be no more than an unorganized rabble, unrepresentative of a population which only wants to live peacefully under French rule and to enjoy the benefits of *la mission civilisatrice*.

That Nationalism without Communism is a force on its own is ignored by those who look backwards to halcyon days of colonialism in the nineteenth century. But the political purity of Algerian nationalism is its main strength. Were it tainted with Communism it would get no support, moral or material, from the Sultan of Morocco or from M. Bourguiba in Tunisia. Equally, the very fact that the F.L.N. is so bitterly anti-Communist shows up in stark relief the portentous opportunity which is being missed in Algeria today. If a negotiated settlement could be arrived at, the whole of the north-western corner of Africa would join in a full and active partnership with the West and in the closest political and economic relations with France. To realize such a settlement there must be not only a change of Governor and Government in Algiers, but a change of heart in Paris. France must act as if she had a future and not just a past.

Chapter III

LIBYA

FLYING from Tunis into Libya is a remarkable experience and a memorable transformation. Tunisia is sophisticated and cultivated, Libya is simple and desert. Tunisia numbers a member of the Jewish faith in its Government; Libya would be hard put to it to find a Jew to put in any post. In Tunis too the veil has almost disappeared with the Bourguiba emancipation laws; in Tripoli the veil is so heavy that no Moslem woman is permitted more than the smallest peephole.

Coming from countries like Morocco and Tunisia where the French social and cultural influence after fifty years of colonization has gone so very deep, it is almost impossible to believe that Libya was an Italian colony until a few years ago. Apart from a few good roads and buildings, the Italians have left little or nothing behind them of culture, language and tradition. Ancient Rome left the fabulous remains of the once great cities of Sabratha and Leptis Magna. But of Mussolini's Italy the principal residue is an indelible hatred, especially strong among the Senoussi of Cyrenaica, whose long-drawn-out rebellion the Italians were unable to pacify right up to the beginning of the Second World War, and with whom memories are still green of the monstrous retribution meted out by Marshal Graziani when—as Governor of Cyrenaica—he ordered all the desert wells to be cemented in. Hundreds of human beings and thousands of animals died of thirst from this diabolical act, known in the Arab code of war as the one weapon never to be used against even their bitterest enemy. It is perhaps not to be wondered at that Cyrenaica, now a part of an independent Libya, permits of no Italian settlement within its borders—the few Italians who remain being confined to Tripolitania.

Nevertheless the exodus of Italian settlers has not helped over one of Libya's most important problems—the desperate lack of population. In terms of simple statistics Libya has one million inhabitants for nearly one million square miles of territory.

True the vast majority of this area is nothing but rock and sand, relieved only by occasional patches of sour thorny scrub. But on the hill plateaus, where the rain is caught by irrigation ditches before it runs away to waste itself in the desert below, the ground is green, the corn crops flourish and the wild flowers grow in coloured clumps of abundance. It is not to exaggerate the limited possibilities of these few fertile islands in the desert sea to say that a little more population, plus a few scientific aids, could produce a lot more food.

As things are, it seemed to me as I travelled about this vast and barren land that it was only by a miracle that Libya survived. Add to the poverty of her productive capacities the constant menace of Egyptian penetration and propaganda and you wonder how Libya can possibly stand amidst the pressures of this savage world.

Libya gained her independence under the auspices of the United Nations in 1951 and in fulfilment of Britain's wartime pledge to the Senoussi that they would be freed from Italian rule. Ever since then the Egyptians have been hard at it to try and subvert Libya. The advent of Colonel Nasser and his revolutionary régime only served to step up the effort. Cairo Radio blares incessantly its poisonous propaganda, seizing every opportunity to stir up trouble and suspicion between Libya and her Western friends, between the Libyan people and their King and Government. The Egyptian Embassy in Tripoli has worked overtime to subvert law and order. Bribery, threats— even issues of arms—have been everyday practices for Egyptian diplomats. Last year the Egyptian Military Attaché was caught red-handed by the police carrying a load of sub-machine guns and ammunition in the luggage compartment of his car to equip the nucleus of a pro-Nasser underground army in the suburbs of the capital. He was expelled, but his underground army lives on.

Most insidious of all is the Egyptian penetration of the schools. I remember how, towards the end of the last war, the Communists always tried to get control of the Ministries of Education in the liberated countries of Europe. Colonel Nasser has taken a leaf out of their book. Profiting from the technical and numerical superiority of Egyptian education and Egyptian teachers within the Arab world, he has set out to turn today's

students into tomorrow's evangelists for the Nasser-type revolution. He has done this far and wide—in the Persian Gulf, Jordan, Syria, Saudi Arabia, the Sudan and Libya. But nowhere
has he met with more success than in Libya, where until very
recently almost every school and college was staffed with
Egyptian teachers.

It was perhaps inevitable that Colonel Nasser should go for
Libya. For one thing, it is next door. For another, the United
Kingdom of Libya is united only in name. The traditional division between the countrymen of Cyrenaica and the townsmen
of Tripolitania is deep. True, King Idris under the influence of
his first wife is strongly opposed to the designs of Egypt. But he
has done little if anything to unite his country to resist them,
preferring to stay in his native Cyrenaica away from his capital,
partly for health but partly out of sheer racial prejudice. His
stout and astute young Premier, Ben Halim, does his best to
keep the country together—and he is probably the only Libyan
politician who can do this today.

Yet for all Ben Halim's efforts, the likelihood is that when the
sixty-eight-year-old King dies, his unknown nephew who is heir
to the throne will not be accepted by the Tripolitanians. The
Cyrenaicans may then break away and the Kingdom of Libya
will become a broken and divided spoil.

No doubt that is what the Egyptians are waiting for. At that
moment they would move in. The quarter million Cyrenaicans
might resist, but with a *coup d'état* staged by the Egyptian fifth
column in Tripoli they would be surrounded and helpless and
Libya would fall victim to Nasser's Egypt.

What price then Wheelus Field near Tripoli, which has the
reputation of being the largest American air-base outside the
United States of America? Nasser would peremptorily demand
the withdrawal of all American and British forces. Russia's
Egyptian ally would then command half the southern shore of
the Mediterranean and be able to offer Russia bases within a
short hop from the soft under-belly of NATO. By taking over
Libya Nasser could threaten Tunisia and would have a common
frontier with Algeria and the rest of French Africa, with unlimited potentialities for trouble-making. More important still,
he would be within a few miles of the new oil fields in the
Sahara, with a fair chance that they will be found to spill over

into Libya, or with the possibility of going and grabbing them for himself if they do not.

If these menacing prospects have not yet occurred to Western statesmen, they have certainly occurred to M. Bourguiba. Hitherto the Tunisians have shown little interest in their Libyan neighbours, regarding them as an uncultured collection of camel-drivers. But lately Tunis has begun to sit up and take notice of Tripoli and points east. If Libya started to break up and Egypt to move in, M. Bourguiba would probably try to forestall Egyptian occupation, at least of Tripolitania. Half a loaf is better than all the bread in the Egyptian maw. But it would be a sad day for Libya and a poor return for the money and effort which Britain and America have spent in propping up this brave new venture in nationhood, if at best it were shared between its neighbours.

The Western powers can and must help Libya to avoid such a tragic fate. Libya, after an interval of dithering in face of the Egyptian threat, is now ready to be helped. Ben Halim was a much changed man when I saw him last spring—and changed for the better. Hitherto we had met when as Minister of State in the Foreign Office I had to conduct discussions with him on his visits to London. Then he was trying to ride both the Egyptian and the British horse, trying to play one side off against the other. Then there was no sign of robustness in dealing with Nasser. But in 1957 I saw a great difference. M. Menderes, the Turkish Prime Minister, described Ben Halim to me as having taken on a new lease of life, and I can certainly endorse his view. Though still on good personal terms with Colonel Nasser, Ben Halim left me in no doubt that he considered the Egyptian President to be drunk with power and a menace to the Egyptian and Libyan peoples alike. He had decided to make a stand against this threat and in token of this he had begun a determined drive to rid his country of Egyptian and Communist influence and to purge his Government of faint-hearts and intriguers.

As a Cyrenaican, he has had a tough time getting his personality across in Tripolitania and he has not been helped by the infrequency and brevity of his King's visits to Tripoli. But he is making a brave effort to overcome these handicaps and, belated though his awakening may seem to some people, he deserves all the help he can get. Failure to support him will only let in some undesirable alternative who will give way to Egyptian pressure all along the line.

How then is the West to help Ben Halim's Libya to resist Egyptian infiltration and to combat these seditious influences? The Anglo-Libyan Alliance makes it clear that Britain will fight for Libya if she is attacked. But, goaded by Cairo Radio, the Libyans are asking for a revision of the treaty and the scaling down of British forces in Libya. In any case British soldiers are no defence against peaceful penetration and subversion. We should do better to build up Libya's own defence—police, army, coastal defence and at least a military air transport system to provide some mobility for Libya's armed forces in an area more like an ocean than a country. Britain has not the resources to do all this. But it is an enterprise which could well be shared between the U.K. and the U.S., the U.K. providing the army equipment and perhaps the pilot training and the U.S. the aircraft. Such money would be far better spent than on the maintenance of a British division in a position where it can serve no conceivable military purpose once Libya has raised her army from the present two thousand to the required ten or twelve thousand men.

Britain can also help to train Libyan police officers in anti-subversion tactics. Such training is badly needed in this embryonic State where the security services are being built up from scratch. Britain, after her experiences in Malaya, Hong Kong, Kenya and Cyprus, is particularly well equipped to help Libya to organize effective security services.

Another essential investment that the West must make is in education. The Egyptians, with their ubiquitous teachers, have a long lead here. The Libyans are bending over backwards to train more Libyan teachers and to import non-Egyptians. The Prime Minister told me that Tripoli University is bursting at the seams to try and stop altogether the flow of students to Cairo. Albeit very late in the day, an Anglo-Libyan school is about to start up in Tripoli. We could do more to help train Libyan teachers and technical instructors. No doubt we cannot now purge all of the poison spread by Nasser's educationalists. But it is not too late to prevent the infection spreading still further.

As everywhere in the Moslem world, the Russians are extremely active in Libya. Their intrigues have even been known to involve members of the Government and protégés of the King. At the time of Senator Richards' visit early in 1957 Soviet activity reached a new high and Prime Minister Ben Halim spent an anxious few days wondering how the visit would go off and how many of his own colleagues were as interested as he to ensure its success. The Russians assiduously court popularity with the mob. Algeria and Israel are naturals for exploitation against the West by the Soviet propaganda machine and the Soviet Embassy in Tripoli takes full advantage of them. At a recent Independence Day Parade the British and American Ambassadors were booed by the populace as they drove to their allotted seats whereas the Russian and Egyptian Ambassadors were loudly cheered. (A humorous note was that the loudest cheer of all was given for a car with a plain red flag and a small device in the corner invisible to the crowds lining the streets. When the car came to a standstill out stepped the Brigadier commanding the British forces in Libya. Not even the most ardent anti-Westerners could refrain from laughing at their mistake.)

The Russians and Egyptians are constantly at work on Ben Halim as well as on his populace. They are very free with offers of aid of all kinds, especially of aid in training and equipping the Libyan army—and naturally they make sure that everybody knows about these offers. Ben Halim bluntly told me— and here I could tell he was not putting on the old blackmailing act—that the issue of how much longer he could resist this well-baited trap and hold the line against the easily misled mob would depend on us in the West. It would depend on how soon and how effectively we could show, by concrete and visible results, that Western aid was helping to strengthen Libya's freedom and independence.

Libya, like Morocco and Tunisia, looks westwards for friendship and support. The West has too much to lose to ignore that look, even if it costs quite a lot of money and effort.

CHAPTER IV

CYPRUS

I HAVE heard it said that Britain is involved in the same kind of colonial problem in Cyprus as is France in Algeria. Having visited both these territories and having had many dealings with both problems as the Minister in the British Government charged with United Nations affairs, I can say with some knowledge and authority that this comparison is completely false. Of course Britain bears a share of the blame for the tragic Cyprus deadlock. But Britain is at least trying to get a Cyprus settlement by other means than the firing squad. It is not unfair to say that, if the French had offered to the Algerian nationalists a quarter of what Britain has offered to Archbishop Makarios, they would have got a settlement long ago.

The real nub of the Cyprus problem is entirely different to that of Algeria. The Moslem population of Algeria is homogeneous, it is Algerian and it is more or less united in its national aspirations. Cyprus is deeply divided. There is nothing Cypriot about Cyprus except its name. In this beautiful beleaguered island you are either a Greek or a Turk. From the leaders of the two communities downwards the chasm of suspicion and hatred which separates them is frighteningly wide.

In accordance with an elaborate and most extensive schedule arranged personally by the Governor, Sir John Harding, I was able, during my short visit, to talk to the Mayor of Nicosia, Dr Dervis, who in the absence in exile of the Archbishop was the leading Greek Cypriot, and to Dr Kutchuk, the leader of the Turkish community, as well as to numerous other mayors, municipal councillors, journalists and merchants. These talks gave me an object lesson of the depth of feeling and of distrust between the two nationalities. Although on several occasions Greeks and Turks were assembled to meet me under one roof, I was seldom able to discuss any political issues with one group in the presence of the other. Directly the initial pleasantries were over and serious talk started, either the Turks or the

Greeks—but more often the Turks—would almost always ask leave of the host to retire to another room. (No doubt, if you never have to argue your case in front of your adversary, it is easier to maintain to the full your prejudices and to depict the other fellow's ulterior motives in the most vivid hues.)

But whether this say-it-alone policy helps or not to maintain the gulf of hatred between the two communities, nothing can erase or alter the fact that the hopes and aspirations of one are as passionately held as they are diametrically opposed to the desires of the other. This is not a problem which can be resolved by the simple device of giving in to whatever is the majority view. The 400,000 Greeks want Enosis, which means union with Greece; the 120,000 Turks want to live under British rule or Turkish but at no price under Greek. For all the talk about freedom for Cyprus, what nobody—or at least no community leader—really wants, unlike almost every other colonial territory down the ages, is self-government and independence.

In these conditions, to talk of self-determination is sheer nonsense. The phrase is a meaningless symbol whether it is applied to the island as a whole or, as the Turks now suggest, to the two communities equally. Applied to the whole island it would mean a 4 to 1 vote for Enosis, with every likelihood of armed Turkish uprisings in Cyprus and, if these were roughly handled by the Greek majority, massacres of Greeks in Istanbul, Smyrna and other Turkish cities. The Balkan Pact would collapse and Turkey and Greece would fall back into the age-old enmities from which they were only just beginning to emerge after the last war, when the common menace of Communism brought them together to bury the hatchet in the Western system of alliances. If Turkey still remained a member of NATO out of pure national self-interest her faith in the friendship of Britain, and of the United States, would be shaken to its foundations.

To be fair to the Turkish point of view, there is more than a little justification for their fears of what would happen if Cyprus were joined to Greece. In the first place there is the strategic aspect. You only have to climb the range of hills which fringes the northern coast of Cyprus to see how close is the island to the Turkish mainland. Forty miles away and easily visible on a clear day the Taurus mountains rise above the horizon to mark the coast-line of Turkey. Suppose, say the

Turks, the island were in the hands of a Communist Government in Athens (not an impossibility by any means in the light of recent Greek history), how could we be blamed for feeling that it was a menace to our security? Do not forget, we have Russia on our northern border and Syria in the south. They go on to point out, as Mr Menderes did to me, that every other island of size and importance around Turkey's Mediterranean coast-line is in Greek hands. Enosis for Cyprus would close the ring around her.

Finally, the Turks point to the treatment which Turkish minorities have received at Greek hands in Greece and in Greek-held islands. In the light of these experiences no Turk would trust the word of any Greek Government that minority rights in religion, education and so on would be respected. Dr Kutchuk and some of his friends made much of this point when I talked with them about the future. "Look how the Greeks have squeezed us out of jobs here in Cyprus, even with you British around to ensure fair play," they said. "Once we held a large number of posts in the professions, but now the Greeks have taken over. Just how much worse would it be for us Turks if the Greeks were running the Government as well as all the business and professional life of the island?" Dr Kutchuk and his friends did not, of course, admit that the Turks had largely brought this upon themselves. But it is a fact none the less that their progressive loss of position in Cyprus would never have been as severe had they not responded in too large numbers to the appeal of Mustapha Kemal in the early 'twenties to return and help construct the modern State of Turkey.

But whoever is to blame for the events which have led up to the divisions and suspicions which today bedevil the Cyprus problem, the fact must be faced that self-determination for all Cyprus, however glibly it may roll off the tongues of capricious Greeks and misguided liberal theorists, is for the time being an absolute non-starter. Admittedly no important international decision has ever been without risk. But the risk of the earth-shaking repercussions within and without Cyprus which would today follow inevitably from the union of Cyprus with Greece is a little too big for any Power to accept which takes its international responsibilities seriously.

What then of the so-called alternative—self-determination
for both communities? Let's be quite clear about this. It is just
another way of saying partition. The Greek Cypriots would
choose union with Greece and the Turks would choose union
with Turkey. As M. Menderes bluntly informed me in Ankara,
the Turks would much rather things stayed as they were. With
a puckish grin on his cheerful, cherubic features, he told me
that Turkish Cypriots were quite happy to be under British
rule and did not understand why Britain was not prepared to
go on governing the place. "But," he went on, "if you decide
you must give up, then our people must have the right to choose
to be ruled by Turkey." He had earlier wrung from the British
Government a pledge that the Turks would have this right in
return for their accepting the self-governing constitution proposed in the Radcliffe Report, which would give the Greek
Cypriots an elected majority in a representative Cypriot Parliament.

Thus Britain has, I am sorry to say, committed herself to
accepting the principle of partition as the price of Turkish ac-
ceptance of a self-governing constitution with an elected Greek
Cypriot majority. There could scarcely be a sillier or more one-
sided deal. For, directly the Turks have achieved partition, the
Radcliffe constitution will have no effect in "Turkish Cyprus".
There will not be enough Greeks there to have an elected
majority. This, if ever there was one, is a case of "heads the
Turks win, tails Cyprus loses". Small wonder the Turks in
Turkey and in Cyprus are so addicted to partition.

This addiction is in no way shared by anyone whom I met in
the Cyprus administration from the Governor downwards. All
of them thought that it would be totally unworkable, even with
drastic and large-scale transfers of population. There is no
simple ethnical line which can be drawn between Greek and
Turkish Cyprus. Drive in any direction you like from Nicosia
and you will find the villages alternating between Greek and
Turkish all along the route.

Besides, there is a far more dangerous prospect for partition
than the administrative problem of segregating the communities. The Greeks would not accept partition voluntarily and
it would have to be imposed by force. The experience of partition arrangements in the post-war years provides little en-

couragement to repeat the performance in Cyprus. Why should
we suppose that, on the day we leave, the Greek majority will
not move in on the Turkish sector to repeat the kind of fore-
stalling action which the Arabs took against Israel in 1948? And,
if the Greeks tried it on, how could Turkey, after all she has
said about upholding Turkish rights in Cyprus, fail to intervene
to prevent this Greek grab?

Even if the Greeks restrained their impulses and accepted
partition under protest, the future is fraught with the danger of
conflict. Partition would by definition create a new international
frontier, and it would create this frontier in an island where for
the past three years inter-communal strife has too often been at
boiling point. Any inter-communal incident which occurred
after partition would become an incident across an international
frontier with all the risks of a major conflagration resulting from
it. Either way, therefore, partition contains all the ingredients
of international war.

What is needed, and needed desperately, in Cyprus is some
solution which will serve to unify this divided island, not to
divide it in perpetuity. What is needed is to get some Cypriot
institutions working as soon as can conceivably be contrived.
The Radcliffe constitution must be put into effect in one form
or another. A Cypriot Parliament and a Cypriot Government
must be set up forthwith. Only in this way can we ever hope to
break down the bitterness between Greek and Turk, to create
a sense of belonging to one independent Cypriot community.
This would be the best guarantee for the Turks against Enosis
in the future placing Cyprus in Greek hands. This would be the
best safeguard that yet another Turkish minority overseas will
not be ruled from Athens.

Can this be brought about? The answer depends on how
Britain, Greece and Turkey use the next few months. Whatever
solution we go for we need Greek Cypriot co-operation; and
that would never have been obtainable with Makarios a
prisoner and a martyr in the Seychelles. On that ground alone
it was right to release the Archbishop on condition that he
renounce violence. But an opportunity was, I am sure, missed
by not bringing him straightway to London for negotiations
about the constitution. Of course, he cannot be allowed back
to Cyprus for the moment with all the emotion and excitement

which his return would unleash. But merely to turn Makarios loose without sitting him down to the conference table has played foolishly into his hands. It has given him freedom to make mischief instead of placing on him the obligation to make peace. By fumbling the conference issue, the British Government have handed the initiative back to the Archbishop. They should, even now, get Makarios to a conference in London—not alone, but together with the leaders of the Turkish minority.

I was in Cyprus on the night in March, 1957 when the EOKA presented and published their truce offer. A mood of anxious expectation gripped the whole island during the succeeding days. It seemed impossible to these peace-hungry people, even to many Turkish Cypriots who had no cause to want Makarios back, that the release of the Archbishop would not be followed by negotiations. Apart from the opportunity which presented itself for pinning him down, it seemed it would be too futile just to allow him to make still more trouble. Yet this is precisely what Britain did. It was a sadly changed atmosphere that I found when I returned to Nicosia a few weeks later. Although the terrorists remained quiet, the prospect of consolidating the truce and turning it into a real peace settlement was dead. The hope-filled air of expectancy had given way to a vacuum of despair.

I do not pretend that any negotiation with the Archbishop then or now would be easy or would achieve a speedy success. Makarios does not want a settlement. Like King Farouk during the early days of the negotiations for Britain's withdrawal from Suez, he has in previous talks imposed conditions which he knows Britain will never, and can never, accept. King Farouk wanted Britain to stay in Suez because he hoped right up to the last minute that a British garrison at Suez would come to his rescue if his throne should ever be threatened by revolution. In all previous negotiations with Sir John Harding, Archbishop Makarios has insisted on being the sole arbiter of the future of Cyprus, knowing that Britain with her responsibilities to the Turkish community would never agree. For Makarios knows also that once a settlement is reached and a self-governing constitution is working his political supremacy in Cyprus will be challenged. There will be other Greek Cypriots holding responsible positions in Parliament and Government, who will be only too anxious to confine the Archbishop to his proper ecclesiastical functions and far too jealous of their positions to admit of his trespassing upon their political preserves.

Yet this is precisely where we could force the Archbishop into the open. Whilst every Greek Cypriot condemned the arrest and deportation of their spiritual leader, that is not to say that each and every one is prepared to leave to Makarios entire discretion to settle their future. It was particularly clear to me when I went to see Dr Dervis, the Mayor of Nicosia, that this dignitary for one was not going to be left out of any constitutional negotiations between Britain and Makarios. Nor did he think of himself in the rôle of a sleeping partner. In my other talks with Greek Cypriots of various kinds I found the same determination to broaden the representation of Cyprus in any political talks and not to confer plenipotentiary powers upon one man, who (albeit for reasons beyond his control) had been out of touch with opinion in Cyprus for quite a time. I do not say that I personally struck any clearly definable anti-clerical feeling, though I was told that this is beginning to make itself felt. I do say, however, that, as was made abundantly evident by the spontaneous demonstration of joy and relief in Cyprus when the news came through of the EOKA truce offer and of Makarios' release, the vast majority of the Greek Cypriots are fed up with the state of siege in which they have been constrained to live for so long and would give a great deal to live in peace and normal conditions once again.

I am utterly at a loss to understand why the British Government have not capitalized this opportunity—and I am not alone in my amazement, as I found in my talks with a number of representative Britishers in Cyprus. With this significant and expectant mass of Cypriots breathing down his neck, I am absolutely convinced that Makarios would not dare to expose himself as the real obstacle to agreement. Why then does Britain allow herself to be portrayed as the one who refuses to negotiate with Makarios and the Greek Cypriots on a constitution which was accepted and recommended by the British Government themselves? True it was rejected by the Archbishop when it was put before him during his exile. But he could hardly have been expected to accept it under duress. To take this as his last and final word is to show very little commonsense and even less regard for human nature. Worse still, it plays into the hands of a man who can no longer afford in the conditions of Cypriot opinion today to shoulder the responsibility of rejecting outright a chance of bringing about a political settlement and constitutional development in the island.

I know that the Turks argue that Makarios either would refuse to accept self-government without some time limit for self-determination or, if he agreed, would use the machinery of self-government (parliamentary and executive) as a vehicle to promote the Enosis campaign. But if Britain played the hand with skill, would the Archbishop have support from his constituents if he refused the offer to make progress where progress was possible? I doubt it, from what I saw and heard in Cyprus. As to the possibilities of abuse of a self-governing constitution, no one doubts that this is a risk. But is it a worse risk than that of continual deadlock leading to a renewal of terrorism? No one can tell, until it happens, what will be the effect of getting a Cypriot Parliament and Government into being. But I draw my conclusions from Makarios' own demonstrable reluctance to have this come about; and my conclusions are that nothing could be better for Cyprus or more salutary for the Archbishop.

In all my talks with Greek Cypriots I did not find one who was opposed to the idea of negotiations being held outside Cyprus, preferably in London, and with the participation of Turkish Cypriot representatives. (I wish I could say that I had found the same ready acceptance from amongst the Turkish Cypriot leaders. The most I got from them was that they would take orders from Ankara—hardly an encouraging response in the light of Ankara's insistence that any further discussions must be between the three Governments and not with Makarios.) The real crux will not be over location or representation but over the scope of the negotiation. Violently as they disagree about almost everything else, Greek and Turkish leaders (albeit for very different reasons) are agreed that self-determination should not be divorced from self-government in any constitutional talks. Yet that is precisely what must be done if we are to avoid continued deadlock, blocking the road to the creation of a Cypriot Government and Parliament with Greek and Turkish Ministers and representatives working together.

The British Government should aim at getting Greek Cypriot

agreement to a constitution on the lines proposed by Lord
Radcliffe and accepted by the Turks. At the same time it must
be accepted by all parties that it is just not practical politics to
agree now on any time limit for self-determination or any
scheme for partition. Both must be put on ice until a Cypriot
Parliament and Government has had a chance to work.

This means that the Turks must forget about partition and
the Greeks about Enosis—in a word, that both should think a
little less about national pride and prejudice and a lot more
about Cyprus. As a footnote, let me add that the U.S. Government must also be much less shy of persuading Athens to drop
its aim of annexing Cyprus. This should not be as difficult or
delicate a task as some people in the State Department believe.
As I found during a brief stay in Athens the Greek Government
are fundamentally fed up with Makarios and sick of the Cyprus
issue which only gives the opposition a stick to beat them with
and can bring them neither joy nor renown. It should not be
asking too much that they should for their part abate their
abuse of Britain and their propaganda for Enosis to give time
for a settlement to work which would get them out of a most
dangerous political impasse and deliver them from the other-
wise indefinite assaults of their parliamentary opponents.

I cannot end this chapter without paying a humble tribute
to Sir John Harding. I hope he will forgive my saying that, if
he had been left absolute discretion in all matters, the Cyprus
problem would be much more nearly solved than it is. One
cannot fail to be struck by the commonsense and sincerity of
this patriotic and selfless soldier who hates conflict and loves
peace with the simple burning passion of an Eisenhower. I was
especially struck by one remark. "You can have all the agreements you like between London, Athens and Ankara," he said.
"But the thing which will determine the future of Cyprus is the
integrity and devotion of the teaching profession in the island."
Harding is absolutely right. This is where British governments have failed most tragically in the past, and from their
failure has been born most of the division and hatred which has
kept and is still keeping the two communities apart. Until very
recently there was no English school for Cypriots anywhere in
the island. There is still no university. All Greeks went to Greek
schools and were taught Enosis; all Turks went to Turkish

schools and were taught to distrust Greeks. Now the new English school in Nicosia is crowded out with children of both communities who are taught to live together.

It is not too late to spread this system across the island, to inculcate a sense of unity in the rising generation. But the governments concerned, as well as Makarios and the other leaders of the communities, must give the teachers—and themselves—the chance to unify and so redeem the island of Cyprus.

CHAPTER V

THE BAGHDAD PACT

AFTER the tragic frustrations and disappointed hopes of
Cyprus it was a joy to arrive in Baghdad. For one thing
the Iraqis were busily preparing for the opening of their
"Development Week" when their latest economic and social
achievements would be on show to the world. More important
still, the United States had just announced, following the Bermuda Conference between President Eisenhower and Prime
Minister Macmillan, that they would, if invited, join the Military Committee of the Baghdad Pact.

Before Bermuda, Mr Menderes, the Turkish Premier, told
me the one thing he hoped for out of this Conference was the
news that America would join at least the Military Committee
of the Baghdad Pact, if not the Pact itself. He went on to say
that the best way to help our enemies and their assistants in the
Middle East was for the United States to go on treating everyone and everything that was associated with Britain as taboo.
The Eisenhower Doctrine was fine as far as it went, but it did
not go far enough. To have real and effective meaning it must
be supplemented by American membership of the only existing
anti-Communist alliance among Middle-Eastern States—the
Baghdad Pact of Turkey, Iraq, Iran, Pakistan and Great Britain. Nothing could be more dangerous or create more real
despair in the hearts of our friends than for the Americans to
accept the mischievous line of argument that it was the Baghdad
Pact which had divided the Middle East. The division had been
created by the enemies of the Pact, by Nasser, who regarded it
as a threat to his supremacy in the Arab world and a build-up
for his rival, Iraq. Did America want Nasser to be supreme? Or
did she think that by cold-shouldering Iraq she would get
Nasser to be sweetly reasonable about the Suez Canal and to
stop flirting with Russia? Whichever it might be, Menderes said
that America's performance in the Middle East since the Baghdad Pact was signed in 1955 had done nothing but confuse and

depress our best friends in the Arab and Moslem world. Mr John Foster Dulles had virtually invented this alliance and had at first roundly chastised Britain and other countries for being slow to adopt his brain-child. Then for fear of Israeli counter demands, Egyptian opposition and Saudi anxieties he had calmly left this inadequately equipped infant upon Iraq's and Turkey's doorstep.

President Chamoun of Lebanon had been only a little less emphatic in the views he expressed to me in Beirut on my way to Baghdad. The worst thing, he said, that Britain and America could do for people like the Lebanese was to go their separate ways in the Middle East and to present a constant spectacle of rivalry, jealousy and misunderstanding between each other. Though he had not joined the Baghdad Pact, he had publicly proclaimed that Lebanon was with the West in the great world struggle against Communism. For this he was being subjected to a sustained attack by Egypt and Syria. The Egyptian and Syrian secret services, aided and abetted by the Russians, were continually at work to stir up trouble in Lebanon. Arms were being smuggled from Syria to the Moslem parts of Northern Lebanon to try to upset by force the precarious balance between Christians and Moslems, and to start up civil disturbances throughout the country.

In 1956 during the Suez crisis this solid friend of the West, who heads the Christian community of Lebanon and who looks like a film-star and talks like a statesman, had shown enormous courage in dealing with what had promised to be an ugly situation for Britain and the West. Bombs had been smuggled in by Egyptian military attachés and thrown at the British Embassy and other Western institutions. The Lebanese Government had panicked and formed up to the President to demand that Lebanon should break off diplomatic relations with Britain and France and steer an anti-Western course of policy.

Chamoun acted without hesitation. He dismissed his Government and appointed a new one on whom he could rely to pursue his own pro-Western policy, he sent the Egyptian attachés packing and he arrested and imprisoned the perpetrators of the bomb outrages. Chamoun therefore had a right to criticize us and to say that, if Britain and America really wanted to help him hold the Lebanon to his pro-Western course, they must

first stop squabbling and show by their actions that they were
working together to support those who resisted Communism in
the Middle East.

Yet before I left London to begin my tour, and right up to
the Bermuda Conference itself, there had been few signs of
Britain and America coming together. The Eisenhower Doctrine
had been formulated in isolation and proclaimed without a
word of consultation with the British Government. In London
the attitude to American Middle East policy was, "Let these
novices go their own way and make their own mistakes", with
no serious regard for the appalling consequences which could
ensue.

The Iraqi Crown Prince had asked me to come and see him
on his return through London from visiting the U.S. in February, 1957. He was full of woe and even indignation at the
American response to his appeal for military aid on behalf of
the Baghdad Pact powers. He had been told that America must
keep a balance of arms deliveries not only between Israel and
her Arab neighbours, but between the Arabs themselves. Was
Iraq, a proven ally of the West, to be equated with Syria, a
proven ally of Russia? he asked. I denied this, but my denial
did not sound convincing.

It seemed the last straw for the Baghdad Pact, the final proof
that the two great Western allies were determined not to be
allies in the Middle East. At the time of the Suez crisis in
November, 1956 the Pact had been all but destroyed. Britain
had been asked not to attend meetings of the Pact's Council.
Pakistan was on the point of quitting either the Commonwealth
or the Pact or both. Iraq was rioting and Nuri-es-Said was in a
minority of one in his Government on the issue of whether to
break off relations with Britain and to force her out of the Pact.
Only the strength and good sense of Iran's Shah, Turkey's
Menderes and later Pakistan's Mirza and Suhrawady saved the
cohesion of the alliance.

Then with the Bermuda Conference came the transforma-
tion. I happened to arrive in Baghdad on the day that President
Eisenhower announced America's decision to join the Military
Committee of the Baghdad Pact. To say that Premier Nuri-es-
Said, when I saw him that afternoon, was like the cat that had
swallowed the cream is the understatement of the year. He was

beaming and purring with joy and relief. When I thanked him for his loyal support at the time of the Suez crisis he made light of the episode. This was the past, he said, and it would be forgotten. It had been a tough time, especially for him with his record of sympathy towards Britain. But for the first time in Iraq's history a Prime Minister had refused to give way to a mob that was howling for his resignation, if not for his blood, and this was something of the greatest significance for the future. The Crown Prince too was a different creature to the picture of despair and dejection which I had seen in London. The British and American Ambassadors looked like men suddenly relieved of an intolerable burden. Gone from their faces was the look of desperate frustration at trying to explain to Washington that the best way to confound our enemies was to back up our friends, to make our allies the success story of the Arab world instead of letting Nasser claim the title. In one stroke the Bermuda announcement had shown that America and Britain were at last playing in the same team, no longer kicking the ball in opposite directions to the delight of the Russians in the grandstand.

Nor was the relief and happiness which this development had wrought confined only to high places. It spread to all sections of the people. When I went to cable a news story to the *New York Herald Tribune* describing the joyful reaction of Baghdad, I found that I was not properly registered as a newspaper correspondent in Iraq. I gave my name to the clerks in the cable office and asked them to read the cable through. Instantly their whole attitude changed. I might not be properly registered, but I was their friend and I was sending good news and they would see that it was sent. Whether the *Herald Tribune* ever got the bill for the cable I do not know; but it would not surprise me if the cable office people paid it themselves, so anxious were they to transmit the glad tidings!

Another example of the sudden change of public feeling occurred on the opening day of Iraq's "Development Week". The project selected for the first tape-cutting ceremony of this week was a new bridge over the Tigris, a product of British engineering. After King Faisal had declared the bridge open and departed, not without difficulty, through a milling mass of cheering, joyful Baghdadis, the British Ambassador, Sir Michael

Wright, drove across the bridge on his way back to the Embassy. Directly the crowd saw his car and recognized the Union Jack they surrounded it, some of them opening the doors and climbing inside to shake him and his wife by the hand, and all the while shouting and chanting "Thank you for our bridge."

Only a few weeks before this Michael Wright, though one of the most popular Ambassadors Britain has ever had in Iraq, found sullen, silent and resentful faces wherever he drove in the city. Nuri had summed it up—Suez would be forgotten. Iraq was thinking of the positive constructive things her friends had done. It was not lost on many of the thinking Iraqis to whom I spoke that Britain, in addition to building bridges over the Tigris, had been mainly responsible for persuading America to abandon her hesitations and to throw her weight behind those who were already committed in the struggle against Communism and who were trying to stop Nasser's imperialism in the only right way—by building up an alternative leadership.

But, as I was quickly reminded by Mr Auni Khalidi, an old friend and collaborator of mine from the Iraqi delegation at the U.N., and now the Secretary-General of the Baghdad Pact, this type of alliance cannot live forever on one boost from America. There must be a follow-through and the most obvious follow-through he could think of was for the U.S. to become a full member of the Pact. They were now members of all the three most important committees, economic, military and counter-subversion. There was no sense in their being stand-offish about joining the Council and so taking part in the political machinery of the Pact as well.

I know well the arguments which Washington has presented for not joining the Pact as a whole. They vary according to which section of the State Department happens to be briefing Mr Dulles on the day in question. Sometimes it is the Israeli desk who tell the Secretary of State that Israel would demand a compensating guarantee of her present frontiers. Sometimes it is the Saudi desk saying that King Saud is not yet sufficiently reconciled to his Northern Hashemite neighbour to view with calm an Iraqi-American alliance. Sometimes a voice from the Pentagon ups and says that the U.S. should not add to her military commitments, and again sometimes Mr Dulles's advisers will whisper that Congress would be opposed on all these grounds to full U.S. participation in the Baghdad Pact.

Of course Israel would make good any opportunity to squeeze a formal frontier guarantee out of Washington. But the more realistic Israelis equally admit, as Ambassador Ebba Eban admitted to me two years ago at the U.N., that the Baghdad Pact is in no sense a threat to Israel, rather the contrary, in so far as it averts the Arab gaze from the struggles within the Middle East and direct it towards the far greater menace from without. As to King Saud's reactions, I found when I saw him that he is far too concerned about the threat of Soviet Russia to feel, let alone to express, any indignation at his American ally joining the only Middle East anti-Communist alliance.

Nor would such a step extend American defence commitments. Indeed the actual commitment would be a good deal less than the U.S. Congress has already approved when it voted acceptance of the Eisenhower Doctrine. Under the Doctrine, American forces are pledged to aid any Middle-Eastern State that considers itself threatened by Soviet Communism. Under the Baghdad Pact the obligation is limited to the four Middle-Eastern members of the Pact—Turkey, Iraq, Iran and Pakistan. With these replies it would seem that Mr Dulles is well enough armed to answer any Congressional criticisms of America taking this long overdue plunge.

Auni Khalidi and his colleagues in the Baghdad Pact Secretariat also laid great stress with me on the economic work of the Pact. They had been greatly heartened by an announcement made by the Richards mission when they visited Ankara that American dollar aid would be given, not only to the individual members of the Pact, but also to the Pact as a whole to finance joint development projects. The Secretariat were critically short of funds to get some of the most important and essential economic plans off the drawing-board and into production. Paper plans could not keep the alliance together and alive. Public opinion in all the member States would require tangible results from their membership or the Pact would wither away. It was not enough to show that the alliance had halted a Russian threat. You cannot eat, use, or even see, a halted Russian threat. A railway needed to be built to link up Turkey and Iran, a highway between Iran and Pakistan. This would

serve economic and strategic purposes. But that kind of project
could not get started on the kind of pittance which is being
contributed by the present members. Britain, for example,
gives only £250,000 a year for economic activities, one half of
what she contributes to the Trucial Sheikhdoms of the Persian
Gulf. Some of the savings from the former £12 million annual
subsidy to Jordan could profitably find their way into the joint
programmes of the Baghdad Pact's Economic Committee, along
with the money which America will allocate for this purpose.
Iraq and Iran might then offer a matching contribution from
their oil revenues.

On the military side there is much too which can and should
be done to put new life and meaning into the Pact. Two things
in particular stand out, and hopes that they may be achieved
were greatly strengthened when America decided to join the
Military Committee. First, it was hoped that their powerful
modern Western allies would help to establish a modern system
of radar defence along the northern (Soviet) frontiers of the
Pact. Second, the Pact Secretariat hoped that steps would soon
be taken to set up a command structure to do for the Baghdad
Pact what SHAPE does for NATO. The member States do not
have to look far for a G O.C. There is one available in Baghdad
itself, General Daghestanhi, the Iraqi Chief of Staff, who, as a
British diplomat with long experience once told me, can hold
his own in any company, military or political, Western or
Eastern. Britain and America have often been criticized for
flexing their military muscles too much in the Middle East and,
especially in the case of Britain, for rattling the sabre to
pressure Arab States into submission to her will. What better
answer could we give to our critics than to place British and
American forces under the command of an Iraqi General?
What better service could we render to the Baghdad Pact?
Nothing could help more effectively to destroy the Egyptian
propaganda line that the Pact was an imperialist trap to render
the Arab States subservient to the West; nothing could serve
better to make Iraq the latest success story of the Middle East.

There was one final question which I discussed at consider-
able length with Nuri and with the Baghdad Pact Secretariat.
This was the possibility of expanding the Pact to include other
Arab States. Inevitably this atmosphere of renewed confidence

created a new sense of superiority. Not only did I find that Nasser's name was hardly ever mentioned in Iraq, I also found that the Iraqis more than any other Arabs took it as natural that they should have by-passed Egypt in the business of making friends and influencing people in the Arab world. It was not so much that they regarded themselves as leaders of Arab thought and action but that they deemed it ridiculous and preposterous that Colonel Nasser should consider himself in the rôle. As was being shown by the recent comings and goings of King Saud, President Chamoun, and the Prime Ministers of Turkey, Tunisia and the Sudan, the centre of activity, if not of gravity, was shifting decisively away from Cairo and towards Baghdad, Beirut and other pro-Western Arab capitals.

Thus, in the flush of excitement over America's decision to associate herself more closely with the Baghdad Pact, there were those Iraqis who felt that now was the time to extend the Pact's membership and to canvass new recruits. Where, they asked, were the Arabs who Nasser claimed were so violently opposed to the Pact? Saud no longer attacked it, since he had been persuaded by the Shah of Iran and the Crown Prince of Iraq that it was the best bulwark against Communist infiltration and not a vehicle to secure a Hashemite restoration in the Hejaz. Morocco, Tunisia and Lebanon were committed to a pro-West line. Only Egypt and her Syrian satellite were hostile.

All this may be true. There have in the past six months or so been changes and re-alignments of the most far-reaching importance in the Arab world. Yet I am convinced from my talks with Nuri, the Shah of Iran and Premier Menderes that the Baghdad Pact should for the moment consolidate rather than expand. To canvass new Arab members might well upset the favourable developments now unfolding in Saudi Arabia and elsewhere, and give a handle to Nasser's propaganda that the Pact is a plot to subject the Arabs to a "new Western (and Israeli) imperialism". By no means all the Arab régimes are as stable as Iraq. King Saud still fears Cairo Radio's influence with his populace; Tunisia is also sensitive; Libya is far too close to try such conclusions with Egypt; Lebanon is poised on a razor's edge balance between Moslem and Christian and constantly menaced by Syrian intrigue and infiltration.

In all our dealings with the Arab world we should realize that volcanic anti-Westernism is never far below the surface. Our friends want to forget about Suez. But, as I found in conversations even with young Iraqi parliamentarians and still more with Arab youth elsewhere, suspicions still linger that, through the Baghdad alliance and through Israel, we seek to re-establish a zone of influence in the Arab world on the nineteenth-century model. The West can still all too easily put a foot wrong and next time it might well mean the end of our friends.

Rather than risk another "Jordan", it would be far wiser to let events take their course, to make a success of the existing Pact, to attract new members by precept and not by pressure. The Bermuda decision bids fair to create the right precept.

CHAPTER VI

DEVELOPMENTS IN IRAQ

B Y far the most exciting and hopeful country that I found in the Middle East was Iraq. This was not just because of all the commotion about America and the Baghdad Pact. What fired my imagination and admiration even more was the example Iraq was showing to her Arab neighbours of how to use the riches of her oil instead of squandering them.

Iraq is busy proving that not all the oil revenues of the Middle East are used to buy Cadillacs for rich pashas. In a speech inaugurating "Development Week" on March 22, 1957, Iraq's Premier, Nuri-es-Said, put the point clearly when he said, "The gold which is being produced from under the earth is the property of the people. It is from the people to the people." And the proof is that 70 % of all Iraq's oil revenues are invested in development. Under the five-year plan which started in 1955 Iraq will spend £300 million in giving to the people a fuller life and a larger share in the national wealth.

An industrial and social revolution is taking place in this Development State. In many ways what is happening today in Iraq reminded me of stories I had read of the U.S. in the nineteenth century. There is a boom-town atmosphere about Baghdad and other cities. But that is not the whole story. There is also a pride in construction and achievement. The money that is made is not spent elsewhere or frittered away to satisfy ephemeral needs or to create wasting assets. It is ploughed back into the earth and the industry of Iraq. It is used to lubricate and encourage a go-getting and get-building spirit among the people. It is invested in a young up-and-coming nation, under a young and deservedly popular King. Faisal II, his uncle, Crown Prince Abdulillah, and his almost permanent Prime Minister, Nuri-es-Said, make a truly remarkable combination of youth and modesty, devotion and selflessness, wisdom and courage. Like his Hashemite cousin King Hussein of Jordan I had last seen King Faisal when he was about to leave Harrow

school to return to Iraq for his coronation. When I met him
again in March, 1957 there was still something of the shy
schoolboy about him, the inclination to allow his elders—in this
case the Crown Prince and the British Ambassador—to speak
first. But when he spoke it was with good sense, sincerity and
with humour. Above all things I was struck by his modesty. I
had expected to find him in a sumptuous palace, surrounded by
a glittering oriental court and a gargantuan guard. After all,
the oil revenues could well have stood it. But no, far from it;
I discovered him living with his uncle in a villa in the suburbs
of Baghdad which could not have contained more than a dozen
rooms, including the very modestly proportioned reception
room where we sat and sipped our Turkish coffee. One of these
days this engaging young monarch will be re-housed in a palace
more in keeping with the traditional style of Arab sovereigns.
But it is his wish that the development programme should first
do a lot more re-housing of his subjects. The spontaneous popular reception given to King Faisal whenever he appeared during
"Development Week" showed that his sense of priorities and
his sympathy for the needs of his country are not lost upon the
people.

It is easy for the cynics to say that the mob is fickle, that today they will cheer and tomorrow they will throw stones. The
"experts" will proclaim that Iraq is no different to any other
Arab State, that it is held together by the army and the tribes,
by the law of force rather than the force of law. But the Middle
East is changing. Force, the army and the tribal system are
giving way to new pressures, new influences, new social changes.
Iraq, with its modern-minded young King, is alive to these
changes, and is basing its strength not on the fears but on the
hopes of the people. The monarchy thrives not on cold feet but
on warm hearts.

About the Crown Prince, I leave the summing-up to a former
British Ambassador who said that Britain and Iraq would probably never realize the debt they owed to this devoted public
servant. It was Abdulillah who, as Regent of Iraq, kept the
throne intact for King Faisal during all the years of his minority
after his father's tragic death in a motor accident in 1940. Had
he thrown in his lot with the Germans during the last world war,
he could have seized the throne with their blessing and handed

Iraq on a plate to Adolf Hitler at a critical time for Allied
fortunes. If he had succumbed to these temptations, who knows
whether the outcome of that struggle for world mastery via the
Middle East might not have had a different ending? Yet in
these and subsequent years, years when to be pro-British and
pro-West was to court the accusation of treason to the Arab
cause, Prince Abdulillah never wavered in his loyalty to his
King and in his friendship to his British ally.

As for Nuri-es-Said, who has headed nineteen governments
of Iraq, it would take a book in itself to do justice to his record
of service to Iraq, to Britain and to the Western world. Wherever
and whenever Britain has found herself in a tight corner during
the past forty years and more she has also found Nuri ready
and willing to do battle, to stake all for her cause. In the First
World War when Britain needed Arab help to defeat the
Turks, then allied to Germany and threatening the British life-
line to the East, Nuri organized, galvanized and delivered the
Arabs to defeat our enemies. In the last war he again resisted
every German incursion. Today finds Nuri the organizer and
galvanizer of the Baghdad Pact, the principal enemy and re-
sister of Communism in the Middle East, and the resolute rival
of Gamal Abdul Nasser.

In Iraq, Nuri has learned one particularly important lesson
from the years of British tutelage—that the strength, efficiency
and good name of any Government relies on an honest, patriotic and efficient civil service. With a Government Service
which fell short of these standards, the wealth that Iraq obtains
from her share in the oil revenues could be reduced to a small
fraction of what actually goes to national development and the
development programme could be crippled. With the graft and
inefficiency which all too often infects the civil services of newly
—and not so newly—independent States, Iraq's name could be
dragged in the gutter with her friends and neighbours. But, as
any journalist will confirm who attended "Development Week"
or, for that matter, anyone else who has ever had dealings with
a department of the Iraqi Government, here in Iraq is a civil
service without parallel in the Arab world and equal in honesty
and efficiency with many in the world outside.

There are other examples aplenty to show that Iraq, unlike
some other Arab States, has not been afraid to apply the lessons

which the West has taught her and to preserve what is good
and useful in the traditions which have been handed over. In
Iraq nationalism seems to have lost that prickly sensitivity
which has so marked—and sometimes marred—its growth elsewhere. In Iraq nationalism is to be found at its best and most
constructive. Instead of wasting its dynamic energy in anti-
Western outbursts, Iraqi nationalism has sought and found a
productive partnership with the West and especially with
Britain and America. Iraq has solved the problem of British
bases. She owns the airfields, and Britain uses them. The British
air squadrons which are in effect almost permanently stationed
there are invited in as visitors to train with the Iraqi Air Force
by special arrangement under the Baghdad Pact. Iraq who, unlike Egypt and other neutral Arab States, suffered the ravages
of Genghis Khan and his Mongol hordes, has signed up with
the West to protect herself against any repetition of invasion
from the North. In the world of development, at every level and
in every sphere from the drilling of the oil itself to membership
of the National Development Board and the execution of the
development projects, British and Americans are working side
by side with Iraqis for Iraq. The Iraq Petroleum Company is
part British, part American, and half the profits go to Iraq; the
Development Board likewise has one British and one American
director out of a total membership of seven, the rest being
Iraqis and including the Prime Minister as Chairman of the
Board.

Almost every week some new dam or highway, some hospital
or housing estate, produced by this combination of Iraqi and
Western resources and enterprise, is opened by the King or
Crown Prince. In twenty years the cities of Baghdad, Basra and
Mosul will be completely rebuilt. In the past two years a
hundred new schools and ten new hospitals have been finished,
and a new health centre that will look like a small United
Nations building is under construction. The squalid dusty mud
huts of the old Arab slums and villages are giving way to bright
modern brick-built houses. Over 80% of the houses are owner-
occupied. This method of spreading the spirit of capitalism is
helped by the Government. A man earning as little as £10 a
month can in ten years buy his own house by instalments.
Power stations from the abundant water power are sprouting

like mushrooms and new industries are springing up across the camel tracks of the desert.

Telecommunications are expanding rapidly, every village now having postal and telephone links with Baghdad. Iraq also boasts the only television network in the Middle East. This is much used for education as well as entertainment and, with the very latest equipment, reception is even better than in many parts of Britain or America. In boom-town Baghdad the products of General Motors jostle and bustle in the dusty crowded streets and real estate in the shopping quarter is worth more than in London's Piccadilly.

Most urgent and imperative of all development are flood control and irrigation. It seems strange that in a largely desert country water can be a curse as well as a desperate need. Yet the Tigris when in full flood carries a heavier volume of water than Niagara. Until 1957, whenever the snows of Turkey's Taurus mountains melted, the brown flood waters of the Tigris and Euphrates would sweep away thousands of houses, farms and villages and even whole sections of Baghdad itself.

To prevent this as well as to conserve water for irrigation, vast dams and miles of canals have been constructed, and still more are building. Nuri told me as we flew over one of the Tigris dams, that the amount of earth removed in its creation was over 60% of the total quantity removed in constructing the whole Suez Canal—and what I saw is only one of a dozen similar projects. The water which has been channelled off now forms a lake of 1,500 square miles. When this has "filled up" it will contain as much water as would supply the whole of the United Kingdom for ten years.

Alongside a part of the forty-mile-long channel from the dam to the lake runs a disused dyke, a commonplace feature of no significance to the casual observer. Yet this dyke, according to the experts, was dug before the coming of Islam in the seventh century A.D. Undoubtedly the idea was, then as now, to control the Tigris flood and to irrigate the desert. But the effort was too much for the ancients and the dyke petered out before it reached the lake. Modern Iraq has succeeded where her ancestors failed.

This is but one of the many links between the ancient civilization of the Land of the Two Rivers and the bustling excitement of today's national awakening that make one wonder if history may not repeat itself. May not a new Arab unity and realm, led by Iraq and lubricated by her prodigious natural wealth, arise amongst the sleeping dusty relics of the empires of Assyria, Parthia and Arabia, with Baghdad, Mosul and Kirkuk playing in the years to come the rôles of nearby Babylon and Nineveh of bygone times? May not modern Iraq by the mere assertion of her economic power repeat the rout of the Egyptian invasion of Arabia by the soldier King of Babylon, Nebuchadnezzar in the sixth century B.C.?

Only time can supply the answers. But the air of Iraq today is supercharged with animation and ambition; the Iraqis are buoyant, vigorous and going places with all the ardour and enthusiasm of a young nation making good the opportunities of the liquid black gold that bubbles beneath its soil. They are writing a story of solid success with which the hollow bombast of Colonel Nasser's military clique will finally vie in vain. Iraq is ready to lead the Arab world in the ways of peace and plenty by the simple method of a good example and a bountiful result.

CHAPTER VII

IRAN

AFTER the uplift of Iraq I confess frankly that I was gravely concerned by much of what I saw in Iran. Comparisons are often unfair, but a comparison of Iraq and Iran imposes itself. Both countries have suddenly struck it rich with the discovery of oil. Both countries are in what is technically known as a state of underdevelopment, with a large number of poor and a large number of illiterates. Both countries are ruled by young, sincere and patriotic Kings; they both live on the fringes of the Soviet bloc and they both belong to the Baghdad Pact.

In short, Iraq and Iran share the same opportunities, dangers and needs. Iraq is facing up to the challenge. Iran, unhappily, is not. If this statement sounds unfairly critical to some of my Persian friends, I can only say that this is the way I found things on my visit and that I should be only too happy to be proved wrong. Any criticisms I make in this book are intended to be constructive and helpful. They spring from a feeling of real friendship for a people whose hospitality and generosity to me can only be described as overwhelming.

I say this because I understand that some of the things I said about Iran and its Shah in an article on my Middle East tour were taken amiss by certain of the people I had met. It was, I believe, even suggested that my article showed that the British Government no longer had any use for the Shah and were backing a restoration of the Kajar dynasty, whose long reign was brought to an end by Reza Shah, the present King's father, in the inter-war years. This fantastic idea was stimulated not only by my having made a few criticisms of the Shah and his entourage but even more because I stayed while in Isfahan in the house of Prince Mahsoud, a descendant of the Kajars.

I can assure everyone who read the article and who reads this book that everything I said was my own personal opinion and in no way represented the view of the British Government. As for my stay with Prince Mahsoud, we hardly discussed politics at all and certainly not the Shah or his advisers.

On the contrary. As I drove in His Highness's ancient but still splendid Rolls Royce through the incomparable beauties of Isfahan, I was able to forget for a few hours the troubles of the tempestuous world outside. Here among the indescribable colour, grace and artistry of Shah Abbas' fourteenth-century capital was a brief interval of peace. The rest of the world has moved on and left Isfahan behind it to lead its own slow and easy life, to carry on the customs, the methods and the trades of several centuries ago. Preservation, not progress, is the watchword of this almost completely untouched and unspoiled residue of the great and good old days of Persia's empire: preservation of the unbelievable blue and gold tiling which adorns the exquisite arches and domes of mosques and temples; preservation of crystal palaces whose walls and ceilings sparkle with the mosaics of a million fragmented mirrors; preservation of low and narrow multi-arched bridges that turn an ordinary river into a hundred gushing fountains; preservation of the mediaeval method of pressing oil seeds with crushers drawn in circular fashion by blindfolded camels—jealous preservation of all the antiquity and beauty of the past is the daily task and resolute pride of the guardians of these oriental glories.

No one with any sense of beauty could question the fitness of putting, and keeping, back the clock in Isfahan. It is when the same principle is applied outside that one smells burning and senses trouble; and that is what I smelt and sensed in the Iran of today. Let us make no mistake about it, trouble is brewing on both sides of the Persian Gulf. In Iran, Kuwait and—to a lesser extent—in Bahrain the seeds of political upheaval have found fertile ground in archaic systems of government and law which take perilously little account of the great social revolution now sweeping through the Moslem world. Anti-Westernism is rife among the masses and unless the rulers of these lands and their Western friends move rapidly to meet the rising tide of nationalist revolution, the lid of the cauldron will blow off and our joint interests will be badly scalded.

As in Iraq, so in Iran too, a large percentage of the oil revenues is earmarked for national development. But, unlike in Iraq, the money just does not seem to find its way through to the development projects. Somewhere in the pipe line either the natural indolence of the Persians or the time-honoured system of graft in their Civil Service takes over and the money earned by the earth of Iran and the sweat of her people melts away into pockets as swollen as they are unproductive.

Only in a few isolated cases and areas, where there has been some local leader with the determination to plough back the profits of industry, has development really taken root. Over the country as a whole, by comparison with what is happening in Iraq, the results of Iran's development plans are pathetically unimpressive and inadequate.

The rich and ruling classes are socially among the most charming, generous, entertaining and hospitable people I have ever encountered. Their gaiety and zest for life, for music and dancing and playing the fool is equalled only by their generosity and anxiety to share their pleasures and their riches with their friends and guests. A previously unknown visitor to a Persian household will find himself not only gorged with food and wine (caviar for breakfast and every other meal), but also, on his departure, laden with fabulous presents from the host's own personal collections. The tribal cult of overwhelming hospitality to the stranger within the gates still operates at full pressure in the households of modern Iran.

Yet where national affairs are concerned the same rich and ruling classes exhibit an indolence and irresponsibility that is really frightening in this day and age. The parallel with the attitude and behaviour of their no doubt equally charming and irresponsible counterparts in pre-revolutionary France and Russia is too close to be comfortable.

When I asked how, with these awesome historical precedents to guide them, the wealthy Persians could be so misguided and short-sighted, I was reminded of the history of Iran. This was a country which in bygone times had been a great empire, which had conquered all of what is now Pakistan and most of the Indian sub-continent. The fabulous jewel-encrusted "peacock throne" and indeed most of the royal treasures in the Shah's palaces were once looted from Delhi and other parts of India. By contrast with these former glories, Iran in more recent times —and indeed right through to the last world war—had degenerated into a country to which the foreigner came with invading armies, not to develop the country, but to deny it to his enemy.

It is not perhaps to be wondered at that these years of being a mere pawn in the game of power politics should have induced an attitude of national irresponsibility among those whose duty it is to build up the strength and independence of the country. Nor can one altogether blame the mass of the people if they look upon the foreigner, be he oil-man or contractor, diplomat or trader, as someone who seeks, not the good of Iran, but the enrichment of himself at the expense of his rivals. To all therefore the foreigner is fair game, someone to make as much out of as quickly as possible.

The experiences of Iran in world politics together with the combination of individual high spirits and collective indolence which pervades her people have produced a nation of get-rich-quick *entrepreneurs* instead of builders and investors. There is a local joke that, whereas in the Levant the normal commission for those in authority is 15%, in Iran where the expectation of life for politicians is less and the risk of not dying in bed is much higher, the rate is at least 25%.

Not unnaturally the widespread knowledge of these practices among the holders of public office has stirred up a great deal of discontent among the intellectuals, the liberals and the mass of the people, especially in the towns, whose poverty, backwardness and illiteracy goes unaltered and unrelieved in spite of the increasing wealth of the national oil resources. (In the country areas, where the tribes are strong, the feudal system still operates and the poor—though their living standards would not stand comparison with any Western peasantry—are cared for by their responsible tribal chiefs.) Fuel is added to this smouldering fire of disaffection by the fact that the Royal Family are known to be waist-deep in commercial activities of every kind. Not only do they possess large quantities of land, they also own hotels, night-clubs and railways. Inevitably this association of the Shah and his relatives with the *entrepreneurs* and others, who are known to take their cut of the moneys voted by Parliament for national development, is too easily represented by left-wing propagandists out to create trouble as proof that the wealth of Iran's oil is being squandered by her rulers, or used to enrich themselves by investment and speculation abroad. The prodigious coups of the Shah's sister Princess Ashraf at the gaming tables of Monte Carlo do not exactly help to counter this seditious chit-chat.

Let us make no mistake about it. Mossadeq was not a mere lunatic phenomenon now forgotten, disgraced and never to be repeated. He was the catalyst of all this pent-up discontent both with the rulers of Iran and their so-called foreign masters who, if they had not exactly bled the country white, had certainly not gone out of their way to give it the blood transfusion it required—and still requires. Mossadeq's strength lay not only in his passionate xenophobic nationalism but in his reputation for incorruptible integrity. In the eyes of many Persians he was not only right but pure. He would rob the rich and the foreigner and give to the poor; and they were on his side. Many of them still are, forgetful or ignorant of how near his excessive and unrelenting nationalism went to ruining the country. Mossadeq may be kept out of immediate harm's way; but he is far from being totally discredited. His spirit and his philosophy live on, a subterranean rumbling beneath the volcanic surface of Persian politics. Combined with the neo-communist Tudeh party, now declared illegal but still possessing many sympathizers, these forces could erupt dangerously and violently again. Next time, they might make a job of it. For, if the discontent that I found goes on mounting and a clash takes place between those who thought that Mossadeq was right and those who profit from their daily 25%, I would not care to stake my life on who would come out on top.

Whether the clash will come or whether it can be avoided will depend on how far and how quickly the Persians are prepared to reform their ways of life and business. There is just a chance that they will pull themselves together in time. The best man they could have to bring home to them the challenge of the social revolution which is sweeping across the Middle East is none other than the present Premier, Dr Manouchehr Ekhbal. The Government which he heads shows a lot more promise of attempting the necessary reforms than did its predecessor under the ageing Hussein Ala. M. Ala is without doubt one of the most charming, cultured and generous hosts I have ever come across. But he had neither the energy nor the health to lead the kind of Government which Iran needs today. Dr Ekhbal, by contrast, is tough, taciturn and enormously energetic. His politics are right-wing liberal. He has held a wide variety of ministerial posts, including that of Minister of Court, the job from which he was promoted to the Premiership. Thus he has first-hand experience of handling the Shah and of dealing with his immediate entourage.

More important still, Dr Ekhbal has the confidence of perhaps the most disgruntled and potentially explosive element of all, the intellectuals. Until the day of his appointment as Premier he held the Rectorship of Teheran University, a key position among the intellectual world. He was much respected by all who passed through the collegiate portals for his fairness and devotion to the service of the rising generation of young Persians. If he can handle this section and retain their affection and respect he may yet save Iran from the convulsions of revolution. From what he told me on the day he took over the Government, Dr Ekhbal certainly means to bring to the running of his Government the same energy and activity that he devoted to the University. When he had submitted his political programme to the Shah that morning, instead of the usual lengthy tract of verbiage and grandiose schemes that never see the light of fulfilment, the new Premier had summed it all up in one simple word, "Work".

If I could feel sure that the Shah would give up trying to be his own Prime Minister and would allow his latest appointee to carry out his simple honest programme, I should feel a lot happier about Iran's future. There is just a chance that Dr Ekhbal's personality and experience of his Royal Patron may be able to bring about this very necessary change. As Minister of Court he succeeded in prevailing upon the Shah to part with a good deal of land to the peasants and to give up at least some of his commercial activities.

But the necessary reforms must be carried a long way further than this modest beginning. The Shah will not only have to contract out of a lot more commercial enterprises. He must get his relations, his courtiers and his friends to do likewise and to devote themselves to national development rather than personal enrichment. This is where I fear Dr Ekhbal will run into trouble and be forced to choose between putting water in his wine or facing a head-on collision with the Shah. The betting in

Teheran when I was there was that the Prime Minister would hold to his principles and refuse to compromise on the issue of reforms. On this assumption nobody I saw gave it very long before he would fall out with his Sovereign.

For all his many qualities the young Shah is obsessed with the fear that his Prime Minister may become too powerful. This is partly due to the advice given to him by his irascible and dictatorial father, Reza Shah, who as a former Sergeant-Major in the Persian Army under the Kajars, believed in treating his advisers with the same angry brutality that he once employed upon the Persian soldiery in his Regiment, and who made his Ministers quail in fear of the royal boot bringing both their interviews with His Majesty and their careers in his service to an abrupt and painful end. But partly also the Shah's obsession is due to the memory of Mossadeq and the humiliating way in which this fanatical old man would order his Sovereign about, even to the point of half-exiling him to his Caspian retreat when Mossadeq wanted a free hand to conduct his own peculiar policies in his own peculiar way.

It is a thousand pities that the Shah should allow these fears and prejudices to rule his actions. For he is no Farouk. On the contrary, he struck me as sincere and serious to the point of lacking humour—and courageous too, as witness his seeing off Bulganin and Kruschev when during his visit to Moscow they complained of Iran's joining the Baghdad Pact. Iran had been invaded too often by Russia, he had told them, not to take precautions and the Baghdad Pact was just such a precaution.

Nobody could have proved more convincingly than the Shah that in the conflicts of the cold war his heart is in the right place. But in spite of Mossadeq's anti-Western outpourings the issue for the majority of the malcontents is not the fact that Iran belongs to an anti-Communist bloc or is allied to the Western powers. The issue is far more the Shah's passion for direct rule and the denial of freedom and progress that goes with it. It is this that is making this patriotic and well-intentioned young King the focus of rising discontent. It is this that will constitute the principal challenge to Dr Ekhbal's prodigious energy and liberal fervour.

If the Shah persists in his ways and Dr Ekhbal fails to move him, an explosion must sooner or later result. Another yes-man will be appointed Premier and the smouldering disaffection among the liberals, the intellectuals and the mass of the people could well flare up into real revolution.

CHAPTER VIII

OIL IN THE MIDDLE EAST

NOTHING could be more dangerous for Iran and for her Western associates than another political and social upheaval. It would be far worse than the Abadan crisis of 1951. Then Britain was almost the sole whipping-boy; then only the British-owned Anglo-Iranian Oil Company was to be dubbed the exploiter. America played the rôle of mediator and the Shah and his entourage sought and were granted refuge in a passive neutrality. Next time, however, things will be different. Everybody will be for it, because everybody is in it—the Shah, the ruling classes, and the Americans, British, Dutch and French who form the oil consortium.

Already there are moves afoot in Iran which bid fair to undermine the generally recognized 50-50 profit-sharing agreements which today exist between the West and the oil-bearing countries of the Middle East. Not only does the Shah talk a little too freely of the 50-50 principle being a purely temporary arrangement. He has been the driving force on the Persian side behind the new oil agreement between Italy and Iran. Under this arrangement the Italian company AGIP and the National Iranian Oil Company are to be partners in an exploration venture covering three large areas of Iran. The first is about 100 to 150 miles south of Isfahan and bordering on the consortium area; the second is under the Persian Gulf, in the neighbourhood of Bushire, and the third along the coastal strip of Baluchistan up to the Pakistan border.

The partners put up equal shares of the total initial guaranty of £1,250,000, but the Italians must put up all the capital for exploration work. This will amount to £20,000,000, to be spent over twelve years. If no oil is found and the capital is exhausted, Italy loses all. If and when oil is found in commercial quantities, the partnership will operate. Further expenses will be equally shared by AGIP and NIOC and the Italians will be progressively repaid their initial expenditure.

The profit-sharing is, however, very different to that agreed to under the 1954 arrangement with the consortium. NIOC and AGIP go 50-50 on the profits but the Iranian Government takes half of AGIP's share in taxes. Thus the arrangement is effectively a 75-25 agreement. Under the consortium agreement NIOC gets 12½% and the Iranian Government 37½% of the total profits and the consortium pockets its full 50% share.

Nevertheless, the Iranian Government claim to be maintaining the 50-50 principle because they point out that under the consortium agreement they do not find any of the capital expenditure, whereas under the new scheme, once oil is flowing, they go half shares with the Italians on the expenses. Yet, this argument hardly holds water, since all the capital risk is provided by Italy, and Iran only forks out when the speculation has become a certainty.

Strangely enough this new agreement has not caused nearly the excitement which the Italians expected and hoped for. The consortium companies are not taking it very seriously. They point to the fact that the areas which the Italians have got are a poor third best of Iran's potential oil resources and unlikely to produce oil in commercial quantities. They therefore regard the exercise as little more than an Italian demonstration unlikely to realize Italy's aim of moving in on the Iranian oil preserves.

Italy has felt shut out and she badly needs to feed her excessive refinery capacity. Mr Mattei, head of the AGIP and a close political friend of his president, Giovanni Gronchi, has tried hard to get in on the prodigious new oil strike at Qum, but without avail, as the Iranians wish to keep 100% of the Qum profits. Now it is said that his latest 75-25 deal is a piece of blackmail to scare the Anglo-Dutch-American oil kings and to help him barge his way into the consortium.

Certainly the close relationship of AGIP to the Italian Government and of Mattei to the Italian President suggests that this is as much a political as a commercial operation. But if its commercial success should equal its political irresponsibility, the writing may be on the wall for the 50-50 principle. Within only a few hours of the formal constitution of the joint venture, the Iraqi Minister of Economics, Nadim el Pachaci, was reported to be expressing interest in the terms of the Italo-Iranian deal and to be seeking an interview with Signor Mattei. As I found in the course of conversation with Pachaci in Baghdad this young Minister misses nothing.

Against this it is only fair to add that for their part the NIOC do not want to see the 50-50 arrangement upset. Certainly they want to preserve their agreement with the Western consortium. They foresee the day when, with the development of nuclear energy and the discovery of oil in places like the Sahara, the Middle East may no longer be able to dictate terms to the West.

Nevertheless my visits to Iran, Iraq, and Kuwait make me more than ever convinced that security of Western tenure in Middle-Eastern oil can only be achieved by some international arrangement. So long as these oil partnerships are bilateral—I.P.C. and Iraq, Consortium and Iran—so long will there always be pressure to squeeze another ten or twenty or more per cent out of the foreigner. But make it a multilateral co-operative of producer, conveyer and consumer States and enterprises with a common price, profit and marketing system and a joint development fund—and the hand of the foreigner in the till and in the directorate will be less visible and his security will be enhanced.

Kuwait might well be willing to join in such a project. The Ruler is beginning to realize that profits bring problems as well as prosperity—inflation for one, in a country which earns £100 million a year for a population of only 200,000, and where the poorest rush-matting hut in Shantytown will have a Chrysler at the door. Having built schools and hospitals and run out of pupils and patients to fill them, the Ruler would not be averse to a Middle East Development Fund syphoning off some of the inflationary pressure. But Iraq and Iran have so far taken a different line. They claim they require all their oil revenues for internal development and financing.

Internationalization of production may therefore be a non-starter for the time being. But a beginning could be made with pipe lines. In a sense Tapline have already started the move in this direction in their negotiations with the conveyors of Aramco's oil from Dhahran. By informing Saudi Arabia, Jordan, Syria and Lebanon that they would accept any arrangement for dividing the pipe-line revenues which the four Governments would accept, they have put the onus on the

producer and conveyer States to agree an international settlement. Out of this could grow, with the participation of Iraq,
Iran and Kuwait and the Western companies operating there,
a Middle East pipe-line authority with powers to settle and to
maintain the basis of payment for pipe-line deliveries. Apart
from any political requirements, the pipe-line developments
now being contemplated are far too vast and extensive to be
capable of achievement by individual governments. Projects
such as the Kirkuk-Iskenderun line cannot be realized without
the backing of international finance. Even if the Egyptian-
operated Suez Canal company is ready and able to expand the
canal to double its present size and tonnage capacity, the
expansion of oil consumption in Europe and of oil production
in the Middle East will require still more pipe lines and still
larger pipe lines. This is not the kind of development which can
possibly be undertaken by the existing companies. In every
sense, political, economic and financial, it is a matter of
international responsibility.

Inevitably the idea of internationalization raises doubt and
resistance among the countries and companies concerned. It
smacks of limitation of sovereignty for the one and of profits for
the other. But there is no other way to achieve the twin purposes which must animate anyone who thinks ahead about
problems of the Middle East and its oil—first to create a stable
investment for the West by producing a state of affairs which
all Middle-Eastern States and their peoples have an interest in
preserving, and second, and possibly at a later stage, to create
a fund from pipe-line revenues, and ultimately from production royalties, which will bring prosperity and development to
the needy. To establish a Middle East authority both for new
and for existing pipe lines would help to soften up the resistance
to internationalization. It would be a step towards a fairer
spreading of the riches of oil, towards reconciling the haves and
the have-nots—in short, it would be meeting trouble half way.

Chapter IX

SAUDI ARABIA

Before I arrived in Saudi Arabia the comings and goings which had centred around King Saud over the previous three months had been intensive enough to suggest in themselves that movements of great international significance were afoot. First there had been the visit of the King to the U.S., and the conversations there between him and the Crown Prince of Iraq. Prior to that King Faisal had visited Riyadh, followed by the Shah of Iran and President Chamoun of Lebanon, and last but by no means least in its import there had been the Richards mission's call on King Saud to discuss the application of the Eisenhower Doctrine.

By way of confirming these signs President Chamoun had told me in Beirut that His Arabian Majesty, alive to the dangers of Nasser's flirtations with Russia, was trying to loosen his ties with Egypt. The Crown Prince of Iraq believed that King Saud was now paying Egypt only enough Danegeld to avoid the attentions of Cairo Radio of which he is still afraid, and small wonder in a country steeped in the traditions of a theocratic system, where extremes of wealth and poverty are as great as in pre-Revolutionary France or Russia. Nuri thought King Saud was fully persuaded of the Syrian threat. So did President Mirza of Pakistan and the Shah who felt that the Saudis would move if the Syrian position deteriorated further. All agreed that the Saudi line on the Baghdad Pact was now benevolent neutrality.

So it was with high hopes that I set off to see the King from the brand new hotel where I had been installed as a royal guest in a lavishly comfortable suite of rooms. I had heard many stories of the hospitality with which the Saudis overwhelm those who have the good fortune to be received as guests of the King. But I was still unprepared for the treatment given to me. Cars, aeroplanes, hotels, meals—everything in fact except liquor, which is forbidden for everyone—were laid on at short notice and no notice. An Aramco Dakota was hired (or requisitioned) to fly me from Dhahran to Riyadh. In Riyadh four new and luxuriously air-conditioned Cadillacs were put at my disposal, one for each of the four days I spent there. The King gave a dinner in my honour at two hours' notice—a strangely unoriental affair of cold meats and tinned dessert, which was almost entirely spent listening to a Palace secretary reading a transcript of the latest radio news bulletin in Arabic. When I wanted to fly to Jedda there was no regular service that day, but one of the King's sons was flying on a pilgrimage to Mecca. So I flew as his guest in a requisitioned Convair—and incidentally spent most of the flight nursing his baby son since the father, it being the month of Ramadan, was overcome by sleep due to fasting.

The only time the royal treatment broke down was on my last day in Jedda. I was booked to fly to Amman. Jordan was in a turmoil but the authorities had just reopened Amman airport. They were likely to close it again at any moment so it was essential for me to fly that day. Catching an aeroplane in Saudi Arabia is always a hazardous venture, even for a guest of the King. True, such a personage is exempt from the risk of the aircraft being commandeered at the last moment by some Saudi Prince, but there is also the time hazard. In Saudi Arabia nobody knows the time; or, to be exact, nobody knows when a time is set whether it is Saudi time, Aramco time or Cairo time. Aramco time is one hour ahead of Cairo, but Saudi time is something all on its own. You set your watch by the going down of the sun. When the sun sets you set your watch at twelve midnight. If you forget you are in real trouble because no one can remember what the time was by yesterday's time when the sun set. All of which explains why, when my aeroplane was ready to take off for Amman, we had everything except a pilot. He had forgotten when the sun had set and could not set his alarm.

There were no such problems over my visits to King Saud. My Bedouin interpreter, the head of the Royal Protocol, saw to that. He had himself and me marshalled well ahead of the time set for the meetings. These took place in one of the many garishly vulgar neon-lighted marble palaces which abound in Riyadh as the principal evidence of the new riches of this Kingdom, which prior to the last world war was a poverty-stricken land of deserts and nomadic Arab tribes.

The first thing that struck me about King Saud was the contrast that he made with the vulgarity of his palaces. Here was the most unvulgar of monarchs. Both in speech and manner he impressed me as a simple, modest, sincere and good-humoured man. I had been told in England that if I was ever allowed to see the King I would find him surrounded by malicious, anti-Western advisers, whose prisoner he was and who would either speak for him or see to it that he spoke for them. In fact, we were alone except for the interpreter who, whether or not he interpreted correctly, certainly did not retail to me anything which was even remotely anti-West.

Everything the King said confirmed and even enlarged the impression which I had derived from the Shah and Nuri and Chamoun that Saudi Arabia had changed sides and cut loose from Egypt. Undoubtedly the Eisenhower Doctrine and skilful handling by the Shah and by the Iraqi Crown Prince had played a part in bringing about this development—the most important and significant conversion which we have witnessed in recent years. But most of all it was due to Jordan, where King Saud had seen the writing on the wall—a message of dire danger from the Soviet-Syrian-Egyptian combination. More than anything else what was then happening—and still is—in Jordan helped to open King Saud's eyes to the red light of Nasser's Egypt and Sarraj's Syria. In everything he said to me it was clear as day that King Saud was putting everything he had of power and wealth and influence into drawing the Arabian Kings' Trade Union closer together and, despite the suspicions and rivalries of the past, to strengthen his ties with the Hashemite Kings of Iraq and Jordan. The battle of Kings versus Colonels was on and nobody knew better the critical importance of winning it than Colonel Nasser's erstwhile ally, King Saud of Saudi Arabia.

Throughout our several hours of conversation the King spoke with a frankness and directness that might have seemed brutal had it not been tempered by a most becoming modesty of manner and an engaging twinkle of humour which frequently illuminated his owl-like countenance. The emphasis in all he said was on his implacable hostility to Communism. He hardly

mentioned Israel except to express concern, as the guardian of
the Holy Places of Islam, that Israel might use her position in
the Gulf of Aqaba to harass or interfere with the traffic of pil-
grims to Mecca which comes via Jordan and the Hejaz railway from the northern States.

During the preliminaries of our first meeting something about
the simplicity of manner of the man encouraged me to weigh in
with the direct question from the outset. I asked how he interpreted his famous phrase, "active neutrality". I got a direct
answer. "Active neutrality, or positive neutrality as some people
call it," King Saud replied, "means not becoming involved in
the Great Power blocs but actively resisting Communism in full
co-operation with the United States and all who sincerely wish
to be our friends."

"How would you apply this doctrine if another world war
should involve the Middle East?" I asked. Again the direct
answer. "If such a war comes, the West will have full use of the
physical and material facilities of Saudi Arabia." Which
suggests that King Saud's concept of active neutrality is more
active than neutral.

His Majesty went on to tell me with much emphasis that he
had told his Arab friends that he would not support any
country—even a sworn enemy of Israel—which got entangled
with Communism. He was also gravely concerned about Syria
and the situation created by the extremists Sarraj and company.
President Kuwatly was not a Communist and he was helping
him all he could to resist Communist pressures. But Sarraj, with
his hold on the army, and Horani and Bagdash, with their hold
on Syria's Parliament, had made a prisoner of the President and
forced him to accept a Government of stooges who would do
their and Moscow's bidding.

When I asked the King if he thought Colonel Nasser's spoon
was long enough to sup with the Soviet devil, I was answered
in one word, for which even my ignorance of Arabic required
no interpretation. It was *"La"*, which means No and was said
with an emphasis of which M. Molotov in his heyday would
have been justly proud. He had remonstrated with Nasser over
the hasty and ill-considered nationalization of the Suez Canal.
This had been "precipitous and unwise" but, as King Saud
seemed to think, typical of Nasser. Then with a great twinkle of

humour he added, "All the more reason why Britain should have shown wisdom in dealing with Egypt to keep her out of the Communist camp."

After these strictures and suspicions of Nasser, the King turned to the situation in Jordan. He had nothing but sympathetic things to say about King Hussein who had the day before removed Suleiman Nabulsi from the Premiership and Ali Abu Nuwar from the command of the army, and was beginning to take the necessary steps to save his throne and his country from Egyptian and Syrian intrigues and infiltration. Somewhat to my surprise, King Saud told me that he had advised King Hussein not to abrogate his treaty with Britain but the then Premier Nabulsi, whom he distrusted profoundly, had won the day. Now he had placed his army at King Hussein's disposal. Saudi forces stood ready to serve his kingly neighbour, even if needs be to help in ejecting the Syrian forces which had entered northern Jordan during the Suez crisis on the pretext of helping to protect her against an Israeli invasion.

In the same vein the King said he had also advised the Rulers of Kuwait, Bahrain and Qatar to maintain close ties with Britain for their own protection. If they preferred to follow the dictates of unthinking nationalism these little States would be lost. He was on the best of terms with their Rulers but his friendship alone could not save them from falling into the Egyptian or Russian maw if they toyed with dangerously shortsighted policies.

Looking back on these conversations and judging them in the light of all that has happened in the six months that have since elapsed, I do not think that I exaggerate when I described them at the time as demonstrating a "dramatic switch in Saudi policy". That King Saud, after Suez and all the propaganda advantages it gave to Nasser, should have gone so far publicly to dissociate himself from the alliance with Cairo and to associate with Egypt's principal Arab adversary, Iraq, is in itself a remarkable enough development. That he should, while his own quarrels with Britain remain unresolved, be actually telling the Persian Gulf Rulers to stick with the British is even more astonishing. Yet while in the Gulf itself I had confirmation of King Saud's assertion.

It is easy to find sinister explanations for this continuing

Saudi attachment to Britain and the British connection. This game of "hunt the motive" is particularly popular among Western politicians and journalists who have never bothered to go and see this country for themselves. From what I saw and heard from King Saud himself, he is anxious, genuinely anxious, to repair the breach that has come between him and Britain over the Buraimi dispute and to restore relations to the same basis of trust and friendship which existed in the days of his father, Ibn Saud.

We discussed all this at great length. Whatever facet of Anglo-Saudi relations we touched on, it always came back to Buraimi. I suggested that diplomatic relations be restarted. "Not till you make some positive move on Buraimi", was the answer. I pointed out that they had been broken off because of Suez not because of Buraimi. Britain had withdrawn from Suez and, if Buraimi has to be solved, we must have diplomats to solve it. I said that we could not come to an agreement with a man who would not speak to us, etc., etc. Every time I got the same reply. The Saudis had put forward proposals for Buraimi but Britain had either rejected them or not replied at all.

It will really be a tragedy if the dramatic changes which have lately taken place in Saudi policy are stultified because Britain refuses to contemplate any settlement of the Buraimi dispute with Saudi Arabia on terms other than King Saud's abject surrender. Amidst the several proposals that have been made for neutralization, internationalization and direct talks between the Saudis and the Trucial Sheikhs, it is hard to believe that some face-saving formula cannot be found for King Saud, who smarts under the lash of a military defeat and humiliation made the greater because his warrior father never suffered the like.

The prize—a decisive step towards the final divorce between King Saud and Nasser—is so great and the moment to grasp it so propitious, that Britain cannot afford to let it slip. Yet this is precisely what Britain seems to be doing, not only stuffily refusing to make any move herself but warning off all her friends like Pakistan and Iran who tender their good offices.

More than this, we are playing into the hands of those still powerful advisers in King Saud's entourage who wish no good for Britain or the West. The Prime Minister, the King's own brother, Crown Prince Faisal, is said to be amongst this group and a bitter opponent of Iraq and the Baghdad Pact. I cannot honestly give an opinion on this, for I spent only a short time with him. He was not in good health; indeed I was told that he seldom is. I found him very different to his brother. Humourless and outspokenly suspicious of everything the West did, he had none of the King's kindliness of manner, though in height, build and face he was the finest looking man I have ever seen.

One man for whose passionate anti-Westernism I can fully vouch is the Foreign Minister. He is an old adversary of mine in debate and negotiation, the Rasputin-like Eminence Noire of the Saudi Government, the sinister Syrian Sheikh Yusuf Yasin, about whom everything rings as false as his dyed black beard. One of the healthiest signs that I found in Riyadh was the extent to which Yusuf Yasin was kept out of my talks with the King and the Crown Prince. Not long ago such was his influence that he would almost certainly have been in on everything connected with my visit. He certainly tried hard, as I could guess from an animated conversation between him and the Crown Prince during the King's dinner. But in vain. Sheikh Yusuf has fallen—at least temporarily—from grace. As the pro-Egyptian, pro-Syrian adviser who tried to embroil Saudi Arabia in the Russian arms racket, his advice is not sought by a King now thoroughly convinced of the Egyptian, Syrian and Russian menace to his throne and kingdom.

But Yusuf Yasin is biding his time, building up his case against the West and against Britain in particular, hoping to stage a come-back on the errors of British policy in the Middle East and especially in the Persian Gulf. He tried in Riyadh to put me through a two-hour inquisition about Buraimi and everything else from which he could extract a few propaganda points. It was a fascinating sight to watch him in action, trying desperately to build up the dossier with the aid of an interpreter who was keeping a verbatim record of what was said. It was a hot night and after half an hour the Sheikh removed his head-dress; after an hour he took off his robe, then undid his collar and finally removed his shoes. I hope he was not very satisfied with the results of this extraordinary night of political strip-poker, though I have to pay tribute to his persistence. Gypsy Rose Lee certainly never worked harder.

With the Yusuf Yasins of life around in Saudi Arabia we cannot afford to take for granted King Saud's recent conversion to
a more pro-Western line. There are still too many prickly
issues that stand between us and him, too many thorns in his
flesh, such as Buraimi, too many areas which he can stir up
against us, such as Oman. We have not yet won Saudi Arabia
to our side, but we could if we really tried.

CHAPTER X

PERSIAN GULF STATES

THE classical British argument against conceding any ground to King Saud over Buraimi is that it would fatally undermine Britain's position throughout the Persian Gulf. We are reminded of how vital the Gulf is to Britain and how we could not do without Kuwait's oil and the Bahrain refinery. From this the conclusion is drawn that we must show strength if we are to maintain any sort of respect and loyalty to the British connection from the Sheikhdoms and the Trucial States. This might conceivably be true if we still had the strength to show. But we have not—at least not the kind of strength which is usable to deal with the kind of trouble that is likely to arise in these parts. Britain has put her money into a nuclear armoury and atomic bombs are not the best weapons to put down a riot in the vegetable market in Bahrain. Even before the new reorganization plans for the British armed forces, the strategic reserve for the Persian Gulf had been reduced to a handful of infantry which in the event of trouble was more effective as an irritant than as a police force.

The Persian Gulf States are a relic of the old Indian Empire. Once India became independent and Britain could no longer depend upon the Indian army to keep order along the Trucial coast, Britain's position became an anachronism. The real danger to Britain's oil supplies today lies, not in making concessions to King Saud over Buraimi, but in perpetuating this anachronism and the present archaic state of relations with Kuwait, Bahrain, etc., which satisfies no one except the Rulers who enjoy the privileges of their own tribal autocracy and, in theory, the protection of British forces.

Under the treaties which govern these relations Britain is in the unenviable position of having responsibility without the power to discharge it. Britain is responsible for the external affairs of these territories, for defending them against attack from without and for restoring the peace within in the event of

a total breakdown of law and order. Yet by the same treaties
Britain is debarred from any interference in the internal administration. This means that she cannot maintain security
checks on people entering and leaving these States. Under a
new law in Kuwait no visas are required for the nationals of
any Arab State. This is an open invitation to Egyptian and
other mischief-makers to come in and stir up trouble against the
West. Britain is powerless to prevent their coming or to stop
them starting a really big fire. Yet should they succeed—and
the Kuwaiti security service is not all that effective—Britain has
the responsibility, and the vital interest, of putting out the
flames with a completely inadequate fire-brigade for the job.

This is not all. The régimes of Kuwait and Bahrain—to name
only the two most important and explosive States—are hardly
democratic by any standard. By the terms of the treaties, this
is an internal affair and has nothing to do with Britain. Yet because the British are everywhere about them—British warships
in the Gulf, British marines often on shore, British oil-men running the oil-fields, British advisers in the government service and
the Rulers' courts—it is not the Rulers who get the blame for
denying their subjects freedom but the British for failing to
force or to persuade the Rulers to introduce democratic reforms.

This is really a fantastic state of affairs and the worst example
I have ever seen of Britain getting herself the worst of every
world. We are regarded as the Colonial overlord, yet we have
no "colonial" powers. For their part the young nationalists who
chafe under the autocracy of their rulers feel, as they told me
with great seriousness but without bitterness, like a colony without the benefits of British Colonial rule, such as impartial justice, freedom of expression and association, universal education
and so on.

Egypt has been quick to exploit this perfect opportunity to
make trouble for Britain in one of her most sensitive spots. In
Kuwait, Cairo Radio has things all its own way. There is no
local newspaper, only an official gazette; so Egyptian lies go
unanswered, Egyptian educationalists and propagandists are
everywhere, egging on the young reformists, attacking British
colonialism, and blaming the British but never the Ruler for
everything that is wrong or that seems unfair or repressive about
the state of affairs in the territory. Nasser's order of the day is to

get rid of the British first; the Ruler's turn will come after they have gone.

The Egyptians have completely taken over Kuwaiti education. For a total population of 200,000 men, women and children there are no fewer than 500 Egyptian school-teachers, of whom at least 400 are known to have been fully indoctrinated and trained to teach the gospel according to Colonel Nasser. As yet there is no university, so all those who want to specialize troop off to Cairo University where they undergo further political treatment.

It is all very well for the ruling family to regard those so treated as a lot of insignificant adolescents. In a very short time they will be a powerful addition to the young reformists, if not to the Egyptian fifth column. Already some of the younger Sheikhs are secretly in sympathy with the reformist movement. If nothing is done to remove the Egyptian menace except to forbid its creatures to foregather in public places, the young reformists will fall completely under the influence of Nasser and the Kuwaiti children of today will develop into a generation of adolescent revolutionaries bent on ousting all Western influence and interests and overthrowing their present rulers.

The ruling family are frighteningly complacent about this threat. Not one amongst them with whom I spoke really took it seriously. To every suggestion that there was a strong smell of burning in Kuwait, they would reply by pointing to the tribal loyalty of the Kuwaitis, in whom they had absolute trust. They see no danger in the fact that, around the circle of loyal Kuwaitis which protects the ruling family, another circle is forming, composed of Palestinian immigrants with a strong anti-British and anti-American chip, of Egyptian propagandists and subversive agents, and of Kuwaiti reformists resentful of the lack of freedom and strongly influenced by Egyptian propaganda. Yet should that outer circle one day close in, Kuwait would become another Jordan, with this difference—that Nasser would win.

True during the Suez crisis the tough chief of security, Sheikh Abdullah Mubarrak, with great personal courage, kept things quiet. But this only bottled things up temporarily. The young reformists and the disaffected Palestinians withdrew to fight another day; and that day may be all too soon.

In Bahrain I found much the same situation as in Kuwait, though it was less immediately threatening. The nationalists got a lot of surplus steam out of their system in the riots over the Suez crisis. Some of them even learned, so I was assured, that it is easier to burn things down than it is to build them up again.

The Egyptians have not got anything like the hold over the education system of Bahrain that they have in Kuwait. I spent a good deal of time cross-examining the charming and intelligent little Bahraini, Ahmad Umran, the Director of Education. In between cups of tea taken in his gaily coloured garden, I gathered that he was well aware of the Egyptian menace and had taken steps to meet it. He had reduced the proportion of Egyptian teachers to a mere seven per cent of the total and he was now sending all government-sponsored students to the American University of Beirut instead of to Cairo, which he considered had gone downhill rapidly, even in oriental studies, since the Nasser régime had turned it into a political indoctrination centre.

I wish that there were more Ahmad Umrans about, both in Bahrain and elsewhere in the Gulf. The Ruler, who received me in his palace strategically placed well away from the riot centres of the city, is a spent and ageing force. All efforts to draw him out about the future were vain. He is not the type that thinks ahead. He is content with the present state of affairs, and his entourage make sure that no suggestion likely to upset it ever penetrates the Sheikhly ear. To His Highness and to his family, who sat throughout my interview in silent approbation of every platitude their father uttered, all progress is dangerous and freedom is downright seditious.

This had shown itself in the reaction of the Ruler to the establishment some two years earlier of a body called the Committee of National Union. To His Highness these men represented at best a bunch of hot-headed Kerenskys. In fact they were more of the nature of the English barons who brought about the signing of Magna Carta. When first set up the Committee consisted of merchants, traders and the like—people who, being more in contact with the back streets of Bahrain than any member of the Sheikhly Court, felt the need for a few domestic reforms such as an overhaul of the tribal system of law and greater representation of the townspeople in the administration.

But despite the urgings of his British advisers the Ruler would not meet the Committee's demands. There was to be no Magna Carta for Bahrain. Inevitably with this failure tempers rose, riots occurred and the more extreme nationalists saw their chance of gaining control of the reformist movement. The Committee of National Union became discredited and, after the Suez riots, was disbanded and driven underground. An open liberal movement was turned overnight into a secret revolutionary cell. The young sincere and genuinely patriotic nationalists were left dispirited, disgruntled and leaderless. They see no prospect of changing the state of affairs in Bahrain and they are frustrated by the lack of opportunity in this tiny island, which was once the pearl of the Persian Gulf but which has long since been overtaken by its oil-rich neighbours, Kuwait and Qatar.

I sat talking to some of them in cafés until the early watches of the morning. We argued about what Britain should do. They repeated the familiar accusation that Britain was principally to blame for the lack of democratic freedom. We should force the Ruler to reform the system of government and law. Then in the next breath I was told that Britain should give up paternalizing the Arabs!

When I suggested that the best thing Bahrain could do for the future would be to federate with Qatar and the Trucial Sheikhdoms, I was immediately confronted with the question, "Who will you appoint as the boss?" I of course replied that this was asking Britain to do the most colonialist act that they could think of, whilst at the same time complaining of British colonialism. Yet hard as I tried I do not think that I really convinced them of their own responsibilities.

I am utterly persuaded by this conversation and by everything else that I saw and heard in the Persian Gulf that Britain must get out and get out quickly from the perilous and anomalous position in which she is now placed. Her essential interests are to keep the Persian Gulf States in the sterling area and to maintain her oil stake. This applies especially to Kuwait whose oil riches have to be seen to be believed. The principal field, which produces some 55 million tons of oil a year worth about £200 million sterling, takes only twenty minutes to cross by motor-car.

Britain can secure these vital interests if she can turn the Egyptian attack and gain the sympathy of the nationalists. If she is to do this, she must first hand over control of foreign relations and defence to the Sheikhs. In the case of Bahrain, which is too small to stand on its own, she should encourage the concept of federation with Qatar and the Trucial Sheikhdoms plus, if possible, Muscat and Oman.

This withdrawal will remove the present dangerous anomaly and so spike the guns of Cairo Radio. But it will not of itself bring security to the Gulf States; and security is every bit as important to them, let alone to Western interests, as is independence. As an essential part of the deal, therefore, Britain should seek a five or six power guarantee of the Persian Gulf—the powers concerned to be the United States, United Kingdom, Iraq, Saudi Arabia, Iran and possibly Pakistan.

If the need for such an international sharing of responsibilities for the Gulf States was apparent during my visit early in 1957, it has become doubly so since the outbreak of trouble in Oman last summer. The painful spectacle of a relative handful of Omani dissidents defying the forces of Britain and the Sultan of Muscat and Oman for several weeks came as a dire warning of what might happen if Cairo were to try and lay on a similar enterprise in Kuwait. It was a timely reminder for Britain that she cannot, and should not, seek to exercise the sole responsibility for defending the Persian Gulf and upholding the rule and the rights of the Sheikhs. More than that, it showed how easily a false or foolish Western move can place King Saud back on the same side as Colonel Nasser.

Britain has a treaty obligation to defend Oman—and Buraimi—against foreign incursions. But King Saud has no such obligation; nor has anyone else. Consequently Britain is continually in the position of trying to keep the Saudis out of these areas, whilst the Saudis gleefully jump at every opportunity to get in and make trouble for the British.

This game of cops and robbers may have been all right when there were enough cops, and in the days when it was generally accepted that Britain should provide all the cops. But at a time when Arab nationalism is increasing even faster than Britain's defence budget is decreasing, the game is bound to end sooner or later in a win for the robbers.

There is only one answer—to internationalize the responsibility for the defence of the Persian Gulf, to invite King Saud to join the cops. From my long talks with him last April in Riyadh, I am convinced that King Saud would not refuse. He readily accepted that it was in Saudi as well as British interests that peace should prevail in the Persian Gulf and that only the Communists gained from strife and bloodshed. His complaint against Britain over the Buraimi oasis was that Britain acted in a high-handed unilateral manner to exclude Saudi Arabia from this area. How could he then refuse to join in a five-power guaranty of the Persian Gulf States with Britain, the United States, Iraq and Iran?

Neither Buraimi, nor Oman, nor any other dispute in this area can be settled in isolation by the two (or three) parties immediately involved. Too many considerations of face arise at once in any negotiation to bridge the gulf between diametrically opposed claims.

These problems can only be resolved within an international agreement which gives to each party an equal standing, but— and this is the essential point—which also binds each party to accept and uphold the international *status quo*.

It is still not quite too late to seek such a settlement for this area so vital to Britain, America and the whole Western world. It is still not too late for Britain and America jointly to pull off the dual achievement of bringing King Saud fully into partnership with the West and of rationalizing and securing the position in the Persian Gulf.

CHAPTER XI

JORDAN AND SYRIA

IT seemed hard to believe as I drove through the majestic canyons of the Jordan valley that this beautiful country was in the throes of a major political upheaval. After the endless harsh deserts of Kuwait and Saudi Arabia, this land seemed so green and kind and peaceful that it required quite an effort of imagination to accept that in the cities beyond the spring-clad hills and valleys Jordan was fighting for her life. It was Easter week-end when I arrived to find, not the barren salty desert I expected, but a joyous countryside ablaze with colour, valleys thick with oleander and wild iris, hillsides strewn with cyclamen and anemone joining with the choirs among the green hills of Jerusalem's Old City in joyful greetings to the risen Lord.

Yet behind this natural beauty and security the battle had begun in earnest—the battle of King Hussein for his throne against the imperialist intrigues of Colonel Nasser and his Syrian accomplices. For many painful months King Hussein had submitted to the dictates of Egypt and to the pressures of Syria. He had bitten the British hand that had fed him and his army for more than three decades. He had renounced the treaty with Britain and rejected all offers of help from his Hashemite cousin Faisal of Iraq. He had fulminated against the Baghdad Pact with almost as great a fervour as Nasser himself. He had tamely consented to his army—the best in the Arab world—being placed in a joint command structure with Egypt and Syria under Egyptian supreme command. He could hardly have done more to allow himself and his country to become an Egyptian satellite.

Then a few days before I reached Amman the King finally struck. In one blow he sacked his Premier, the serpentine stooge of Cairo, Suleiman Nabulsi, who had threatened to become the Kerensky of Jordan, and removed the vain, unscrupulous and overweeningly ambitious General Ali Abu Nuwar from the post of Chief of the General Staff, into which he had intrigued his

way after General Glubb had been removed. King Hussein had
found out a little too much of the conspiracies which were being
hatched against him. His reward for serving Colonel Nasser's
purposes so faithfully was to be either dethroned or assassinated.

Exactly when this alarming home-truth penetrated to the
King is difficult to say. More than likely it was a while or so
before he actually dismissed the two principal conspirators from
office. But of one thing I am absolutely sure. King Hussein decided to strike the moment that he knew King Saud would
back him up. The awakening in Riyadh was the turning point
in Amman. Hussein, once he realized that his life and throne
and country were at stake, was ready to take on the combination of Egyptian infiltration and Syrian armed force. But he
could not battle against Saudi cash as well. Remove that from
Nasser's side of the scale, however, and add it plus the offer of
Saudi forces to Jordan's strength and King Hussein was ready
and willing to do battle with all the courage of his grandfather,
King Abdullah, and all the ruthless determination of a tribal
leader fighting for his tribe.

When I met the King, the battle was only a few days old. I
was immensely impressed by what I saw. To say that he had
developed since our last meeting in London, two years before,
would be a gross understatement. He was completely trans-
formed—there is no other word for it. Before the thing that
struck me first and foremost about him was his diminutive
stature. Now it was not his lack of height, but the depth and
determination of his voice, that commanded attention. Apart
from that I was astonished by the calm and coolly calculating
manner with which he faced up to this critical challenge, the
matter-of-fact way he would relate the latest report that Abu
Nuwar, who had just fled to Syria, was plotting his assassination
and an armed uprising with the Syrian forces in north Jordan
as its spearhead. The boy King had suddenly become a man.
He had rid, or was about to rid, himself of the enemies within
his gates and he had the absolute loyalty of the Bedouin regi-
ments to help him resist the enemies without.

As I left the King and descended into the town, I felt a surge
of admiration for this lonely young man, perched in his hill-top
palace high above the turmoil of the streets and markets of
Amman, planning with all the coolness of a seasoned soldier the

battle of his life. I felt, too, a new confidence in the sight of the Bedouin troops of the 1st Armoured Regiment which had been called in to defend their King and keep order in the city. Those patrolling the streets had blacked their faces in accordance with that ancient tribal custom which is designed to protect the wearer from recognition in the act of killing to avenge a wrong. The import of this act was certainly not lost on the Palestinian mob whose faces turned several shades paler every time they came in contact with this awesome sign. Hence the story of a pro-Egyptian demonstrator at the height of the crisis who was running down the street shouting republican slogans. As he came to a corner he shouted "Long live ..." but the next word died in his throat as he came face to face with a black-faced Bedouin. "Long live who?" demanded the Bedouin. Terror-struck, the demonstrator stuttered, "It hasn't been decided yet!"

As I write, some six months after my visit to Jordan, the battle which began then is still raging. It will probably continue for some time to come. Nasser has too much at stake to give up easily. Besides, he has at least one important advantage. He knows that King Hussein is King only of a minority—the Bedouins, who total about 30% of the population. The other 70% are Palestinians—mostly from the West bank—more than half of whom are Arab refugees from Israel. Out of Jordan's total population of a million and a half, about six hundred thousand are refugees. Apart from the fact that they owe no loyalty to a Hashemite King from the East bank, these Palestinians are the most combustible material in the Middle East, and Nasser knows how to exploit them. So do the main parties —the National Socialists, left-centre, the Baathists, Syria's stooges, and the outright Communists—all of which have their own mob whom they can call out at will.

Numerically and politically, therefore, the scales are weighted against the King. Had he continued his attempts to govern through Parliament, he would undoubtedly have been defeated. Almost to a man the political parties and the professional politicians were for abetting or at least appeasing Nasser. The King had no alternative but to dissolve Parliament and the parties and to fight it out with his enemies in the manner of a tribal chief. The sheer impossibility last April of getting a parliamentary majority for a Prime Minister who supported the Eisenhower Doctrine was in itself more than ample justification for direct rule at this time of national emergency.

Apart from anything else the dissolution of Parliament was an essential preliminary for the neutralization of Nabulsi. When I later saw Colonel Nasser in Egypt he protested that he was no friend of Nabulsi. "In fact," he added, "I have only seen him once." I laughingly replied that once was enough for me too. And so it was. Had it not been that I was accompanied by the British Ambassador, Charles Johnston, I confess that I should have lost my temper before the interview was over. Nabulsi was the epitome of obsequious servility to his Egyptian masters and paymasters; and undisguised hostility, suspicion and bitterness towards the West. This was particularly evident in his references to America. He would have none of the Eisenhower Doctrine, which he regarded as America's slogan for imposing her imperialist domination on the Arabs. "Jordan has only recently emerged from Britain's tutelage as a truly independent State. The tender shoot of our newly-won independence will wither in the shadow of dependence upon America's so-called charity," he said. Nabulsi preferred aid from Big Brother Nasser, and he left me in no doubt that, if left at liberty to do so, he fully intended to use his position as leader of the majority leftist bloc with the casting vote in Jordan's Parliament to frustrate any move by the King to seek American aid.

With the parties and the Palestinians against him, Hussein's life and throne depend on three things—the loyalty of the army, the support of his Hashemite cousin, King Faisal of Iraq, and the help of the forces which King Saud has put at his disposal. Forecasts are always dangerous in Middle East politics. Yet I would say that, barring a bullet, the King's chances of victory in this contest are a shade better than even. But this is subject to two important provisos—first, that the Israelis stay put and do not try to cash in on Jordan's preoccupations with her Arab adversaries to snatch any more territory, and second, that the King is not embarrassed by the attentions of his friends.

The chances of the Israelis keeping quiet are fairly good. Prime Minister Ben Gurion seemed to have got the point well in mind when I talked with him in Jerusalem about the position in Jordan. I wish I could feel equally happy that the second

proviso will be fulfilled. The fanfare of near-hysterical publicity
which has attended every American move to support Hussein
and to attack Syria has caused as much nervousness to loyal
Jordanians as have the machinations of the King's worst
enemies. The ill-timed and highly dramatized dash of the Sixth
Fleet to the Eastern Mediterranean when the crisis first broke
caused consternation among those closest to Hussein. More
recently the much publicized delivery of American arms to
enable Jordan to defend herself against Syria has again put the
King in a difficult spot. He cannot appear as an American
stooge, nor can he accept arms labelled "For use against Syria".
He must say that they are to defend Jordan against Israel, not
against any fellow Arab. This inevitably sets up a reaction in
Tel Aviv; the Israelis seek assurances that this is not the United
States' purpose; and, when Washington gives that assurance, as
it must do as a signatory of the Tripartite Declaration, most if not
all of the goodwill dividend which the arms have brought to
America is lost.

Of course we must help Jordan (and Lebanon) to meet the
Soviet-sponsored threat from Syria and Egypt. But it is neither
necessary nor politic to stage a diplomatic reception, with the
full publicity treatment, every time a consignment of American
arms is flown into Jordan.

The Russians themselves learned this lesson in 1956 after
their much-vaunted arms deliveries to Egypt had scared the
daylights out of King Saud of Saudi Arabia and other erstwhile friends of President Gamal Abdul Nasser. Since then the
Russians have said little or nothing about the weapons they
have sent to Egypt, Syria and Yemen. They have not lost by
their silence.

The most important thing I ever learned about the Middle
East is not to get hysterical about it. Of course, we should help
our friends, but we should do so quietly. Of course we know that
Syria is a menace; but let our friends make the noise about it,
not the State Department or the Foreign Office.

The only constructive suggestion that I was able to wring
from Pandit Nehru when he spoke about the Middle East in
New Delhi last April was to this effect:

"You of the West talk much too much about Communism in
the Middle East. The help you give is all given to resist Com-

munism. If that is your purpose, that is your affair, but keep quiet about it. Give your help for whatever reason you wish, but say to the Arabs that it is given to maintain their independence."

This is good advice and both Washington and London would be well advised to heed it.

However well-intentioned Washington's policy may have been towards King Hussein the story of American support for Jordan over the last five or six months has given too many handles to our enemies. It has brought dangerous reminders to unthinking Arabs of the build-up and excuses for the Anglo-French intervention at Suez last autumn. Nasser himself, not to speak of Cairo and Damascus (and Moscow) radios, has been quick to exploit this opportunity to portray American aid as designed to suppress Arab nationalism.

This in its turn has sent our best friends trundling off to Damascus to comfort their Arab brothers. King Saud has found it politic, though I have no doubt highly distasteful, to visit Syria and to reassure President Kuwatly that he will not countenance the use of force. Even Iraq has thought it necessary to join in the chorus of reassurance to Syrian leaders with whose politics she has no more in common than the West.

To the policy-planners of London and Washington it may be more convenient to portray the Middle East in starkly contrasting hues of blacks and whites, the blacks to be ostracized, the whites to be organized. But the Arabs see the conflict differently. They do not want to be organized, and they do not want Syria to be ostracized. They want to keep her in the fold of the family. King Saud made it very clear to me when we talked of Syria that his instinct was to go to her aid and pull her back from the Soviet trap, not to abandon her or push her further in.

This family sentiment extends to a reluctance, except in the very last resort, to admit publicly a disagreement with a fellow Arab State. I remember when President Kuwatly came to Saudi Arabia at the beginning of the Jordan crisis, King Saud first wished to avoid meeting him and decamped on a pilgrimage to Mecca, hoping not to be forced into an argument. Kuwatly, however, insisted on a meeting and in the ensuing discussion was told by Saud to remove the Syrian forces which were threatening King Hussein from North Jordan. Kuwatly refused and an argument followed in which the King and the

President found themselves in disagreement on all counts. At the end of the meeting Kuwatly suggested issuing a communiqué, as had been done on all previous occasions. But, so one of the King's ministers told me, Saud refused on the grounds that they had agreed on nothing and he was not prepared to make their discords a matter of public knowledge.

These are the kind of susceptibilities which guide Arab actions and which Western policy-makers must be careful to take into account. When Arabs, such as Iraq or Saudi Arabia, indulge them, it is not to say that they are any less resolute in their opposition to Communism or any less concerned about those of their brethren who appear to be swayed by Communist influence. On the contrary, it means that they are trying to cope with the menace on their own doorstep in their own way. The inevitable result of supercharging the atmosphere of crisis with sudden moves and counter-moves, especially when directed against an Arab State, is to make the present situation a trial of strength for the Eisenhower Doctrine. This is highly dangerous, for the simple reason that in this way you cannot win. If Nasser and Syria come out on top and King Hussein falls or gives in, the whole American position—indeed the whole Western position in the Middle East—lies in ruins. If the advance of Communism is checked on the Syrian border and King Hussein survives, it will be represented as a victory of Western imperialism and its stooges. Playing the hand as we are doing, if we lose, we are out. If we win, it will bring more resentment than jubilation from our friends whom we only sought to help.

The purpose of the Eisenhower Doctrine must be to help our Arab friends to beat the Communist threat, not to demonstrate the power (or the weakness) of the United States in the Middle East. With a little more tact, and a lot less noise, we can still make it achieve these ends.

If we can do this in Jordan, we may well be doing more than just helping King Hussein to survive. What happens in Jordan will greatly influence the future course of events across her northern border. The history of Syrian politics has always been one of violent swings from one extreme to another. Syria has usually taken sides with a vengeance and a vehemence far more extreme than any other Middle-Eastern State. Today a left-wing minority has seized power and made a virtual prisoner of the President, Shukri al-Kuwatly. Neither in the country at large nor even in the army has this left-wing group any real political depth or following. Yet, backed by Soviet arms and with the hypnotic power of Nasser's success story to aid them, they have succeeded in cowing the mass of the people and the majority of the politicians.

But Syria is a poor country. Apart from a fairly prosperous agriculture her main source of revenue is derived from the geographical accident that places her across the route of the main pipe lines that flow from her oil-rich neighbours to the Mediterranean sea. Syria and Syrian politicians particularly are not averse to the idea of supplementing a meagre income with a subsidy or two from across the border. If King Hussein survives his struggle he will do much to destroy in Syria the legend of Nasser's invincibility and to remove that element of hypnosis by which Syria's present leaders maintain themselves in power. We may all then wake up and find that Jordan has more friends than enemies in Damascus who, with the aid of a reasonable subsidy from Iraq or Saudi Arabia, would be prepared to topple over the left-wing minority which is now in office. Kuwatly, as his unsuccessful effort to get rid of Sarraj showed, would change sides tomorrow if he dared. A victory for Hussein might well be the signal for the considerable latent discontent in the army and elsewhere to boil over, and for yet another Syrian Colonel—Nafouri, the Director of Operations—to oust his rival Sarraj and the left-wing leaders Horani and Bagdash.

Such a move could not come too soon. Damascus, when I was there, had the sinister atmosphere of a typical Communist satellite. It was impossible to talk to anyone alone; there was always a third party present. The Prime Minister, Sabri el Assali, gave me an hour of the Soviet gramophone record in its rudest and most violent form, boasting that when I entered the room he had been signing cheques for more Soviet armaments. "The Russians are our friends," he said; "the Eisenhower Doctrine would make us America's prisoner, it would destroy our positive neutrality." When I retorted that King Saud, who thought that he invented the phrase "positive neutrality", was taking large quantities of American aid and had no dealings with Russia, there was no reply.

With the pressures at work today in the Middle East it is difficult to see how either Syria or Jordan can long remain fully independent States. The cancer of Syrian Communism cannot be insulated with safety for its neighbours, as Lebanon, Jordan and Iraq are now finding out. In Jordan, King Hussein must split his country to hold his throne. To make a fight of it he must set Bedouin against Palestinian—the minority against the majority. Without a Palestine settlement (which is as far away as ever) Jordan must remain an impoverished artificial State supporting a population of which over a half is disloyal and over a third unproductive. Under present circumstances, therefore, the only arrangement which seems likely to bring about any lasting stability is for Saudi Arabia and Iraq between them to take Jordan and Syria under their wing.

Colonel Sarraj has clearly sensed that some move of this kind is in the wind. Hence his continued efforts to depose or murder Hussein and set up a united Syrian-Jordan republic with himself as premier and Abu Nuwar as Commander-in-Chief. From what I hear in Iraq and Saudi Arabia, Sarraj may well have drawn the right conclusion. Something of this kind is now very present in Iraqi and Saudi minds, and no doubt has figured in the increasingly frequent meetings between the two Kings and their advisers. When I was in Baghdad there was talk of co-ordinating action with King Saud to form an Iraqi-Syrian Union. In Jedda responsible Saudis spoke to me of a possible deal under which King Saud would recognize Iraq's Crown Prince as King of Syria in return for the Hashemites renouncing any claims to the Hejaz and for Iraq agreeing to King Saud taking Jordan under his wing.

Only a year ago such ideas would have been unthinkable in the climate of suspicion which pervaded Iraqi-Saudi relations. Yet it is now possible that something of this kind will be agreed between Baghdad and Riyadh. Let us hope so. For, as my Saudi friends pointed out, nothing could better deflate Nasser's influence or more effectively baulk his aims. Perhaps, too, only this can save Syria from the clutches of Moscow. At any rate it would mark the end of the long feud between Hashemite and Saudi and an important step towards Arab unity.

CHAPTER XII

ISRAEL

So many words have been written in so many books and articles to portray the State of Israel that I hesitate to inflict upon the reading public yet another description. To me it is a land of greater paradox and contrast than anything I have ever seen. Probably the most polyglot community in the world, it is at the same time the most fiercely nationalistic. Its politics and its people are steeped in the Old Testament, yet largely atheist. Its foreign policy reflects a national neurosis of the most extreme kind, yet when it comes to fighting there is no more courageous nation on earth. As for the national way of life, it is at one and the same time more Communist than Soviet Russia, more Fascist than pre-war Italy, and more democratic than the United States of America. The self-sacrifice demanded by the life of the Kibbutzes would daunt even the keenest collective farmer in Russia; the universality of military service would have been far too universal for Fascist Italy which for all its vaunted militarism still believed in the doctrine that a woman's place is in the home and not behind a Bren-gun; the ferocity with which the Israelis conduct the everlasting argument about politics, national and international, would make even the most enthusiastic American, British or French political partisan grow weary of the subject and yearn for a detective story.

This was my impression of Israel from David Ben Gurion downwards—a proud, prickly and passionate collection of people determined to assert their rights and to establish their nation according to the Old Testament. By pure coincidence I arrived in Tel Aviv on Independence Day, 1957. It seemed the whole Israeli population had come to town that day to celebrate the recent military defeat of Colonel Nasser's forces in Sinai. The Kibbutzes had spilled out their joyful inhabitants to go and cheer their victorious army. French Mystère jet fighters screamed overhead—the pride of the Israeli Air Force—as rank after rank of soldiers, male and female, marched past the saluting base. Behind them to the greatest cheer of all came the captured war material which Nasser's routed army had left behind—Russian tanks, some British Centurions, Russian mobile guns, half-tracks and machine-gun carriers.

When it was over, Ben Gurion spoke to his exultant followers. "We have shattered the Egyptian sword that was suspended over our heads." That was the keynote of the nation's mood in May, 1957, relief and renewed confidence in themselves. In 1956 Israel had feared attack. In vain had I told the Israeli Ambassador in London that no Arab State would risk a second defeat at Israel's hand, no matter what they might say for propaganda effect. The national neurosis had triumphed over logic; Israel had been too afraid of her neighbour's threats to rationalize the chances of their ever carrying them out. But that was in 1956. Since then the Sinai adventure had steam-rollered Nasser's best troops—as he himself admitted privately to me. In 1957 Israel was confident, even in the flush of victory a little cocksure.

This State, conceived in the violence of persecution, born in the violence of conflict and tempered in the violence of siege, had proved that the best equipped of its enemies was no match for its own forces. And Ben Gurion's relaxed attitude as we talked afterwards of the future bore eloquent testimony of Israel's new-found strength and optimism.

Dressed in his usual open-necked shirt, this dedicated socialist son of Russia—steeped like all his compatriots in the Old Testament—summed up Israel's needs as "immigration and irrigation". He told me he hopes by immigration to increase Israel's population to four million—about double the present figure, with an army of 500,000 raised and recruited on the same basis as at present, regulars and militia. This, he said, would give Israel absolute security against all comers, separate or combined. There was plenty of room and plenty of work within the present frontiers to settle this number, given irrigation for the Negev.

Ben Gurion did not say where he hoped to find the extra 2,000,000 Jews. He admitted that the most he could comb out of the two remaining reservoirs—North Africa and Eastern Europe—was 500,000. (By secret agreement with Poland's

Gomulka, Israel is taking the remaining 45,000 Polish Jews, which puts the immigration figure for 1957 up to 100,000.) To make up the other one and a half million Russia would have to open her gates, and not even Ben Gurion could suggest how she could be brought to this unprecedented step. He did, however, say that there was no need for Israel to extend her frontiers to absorb this population. But equally there could be no question of Israel conceding any of the territory she now occupied for the sake of a settlement with her Arab neighbours. Israel needed every square inch of this ground and she meant to keep it.

Since Israel had just shown that she could hold on to it, I felt that there was no useful purpose to be served in pursuing with Ben Gurion the possibility of territorial concessions. I tried another tack, pointing out that in my travels through the Arab world I had found an even greater obstacle to a settlement than the Arab demand that Israel should move back to the 1947 frontiers, laid down by the United Nations. This was the fear that unlimited immigration would lead irresistibly to Israel expansion at their expense. Even if they were not afraid of military attack, many Arabs were all too conscious of the superior efficiency of the Israelis. There was a lot of evidence to show that the motive behind the Arab economic boycott of Israel was more fear of Israeli competition and of the infiltration of capital than national or racial prejudice. "The Jews took our land and now they want to take our businesses" was, I found, a much used argument among the Arabs.

I therefore put it to Ben Gurion, if there could be no territorial concession, could not Israel offer the Arabs some reassurance on the score of immigration? To say that her aim was to double her present population, when nobody knew how it could be done or where the extra Jews could be found and released, was surely to create an unnecessary added anxiety for Israel's Arab neighbours.

Ben Gurion's retort was vehement and unhesitating. In the first place, he said, the Arabs should be ashamed of themselves if they are so afraid of a couple of million or even four million Jews. But apart from that, there could be no question of limiting immigration. This would be contrary to the historical rights of the Jewish people enshrined in the Old Testament. As with everyone else whom I spoke to in Israel, this assertion of Biblical substantiation was the end of the argument. It was also for me the end of the last little ray of hope that I had nursed for a general settlement between Jew and Arab in anything like the early future.

What then is the future of Israel? She has proved her immediate superiority in arms over her most powerfully armed neighbour. But in the long run of the years to come can this extraordinary adventure in Statehood keep up sufficient momentum to survive against the sheer weight of already overwhelming and yearly increasing Arab numbers?

Certainly Israel today is fired with the fierce idealism of youth. Youth runs the Kibbutzes—the average age of one I visited near Gaza was 25. Youth built the Elath-Beersheba oil pipe line in a few months. Youth has turned Israel into an armed labour camp, a militarist democracy where all including the women are soldiers as well as farmers. Israel's backbone is pioneering youth, with all its intensity of feeling and prickly intolerance. As a Western diplomat put it to me, in Israel there are two viewpoints, the Israeli viewpoint and the wrong one.

But what happens when Israel becomes middle-aged and immigration dries up? Will the "married monastery" existence of the Kibbutzes be tolerable to older people? Will succeeding generations be ready to live apart from their children and accept indefinitely the life of a subsidized worker earning £5 a year pocket money? There is also a danger that the European element may become swamped by the Levantines and that re-migration to Europe and America will remove the bulk of the Western technicians and professional men. Ben Gurion confessed to me that this was a constant worry. Between 1952 and 1954 emigration had exceeded immigration and the emigrants were almost entirely Europeans. With so much uncertainty about migration, one can only say of Israel's future that by the time the bloom of spring wears off, the roots of the plant will be deep in the ground. "What we have we hold, for it is our right by the Old Testament", is Israel's motto today and she will fight to keep it so for tomorrow.

To sum up the debits and credits for the future, on the credit side Israel has recently learned two lessons of supreme importance. Israel has learned from her Sinai foray, first, that she is infinitely stronger than the strongest of the Arab neighbours, and second—a lesson equally salutary—that a country in her position cannot get away with wantonly grabbing a piece of somebody else's territory and trying to hold on to it. But on the debit side Israel has not learned any real comprehension of the psychology of the Arabs amongst whom she has chosen to live. Perhaps this is inevitable in a nation whose leaders at almost every level in the State are Europeans who recently migrated to Israel. But inevitable or not, it certainly does not help towards an Arab-Israel settlement.

My first experience in Israel of this lack of understanding of the Arab world was when I visited the Kibbutz nearest to the Gaza strip. The leader of the settlement was a young Englishman of 25. He and a number of young English Jews had been recently brought into this Kibbutz because it was felt that its original Roumanian element was getting a little old—their average age being around 28! The English contingent crowded round me, plying me with questions about Nasser, and Jordan and Syria. "Tell us," said the Kibbutz leader, "is Nasser a Fascist dictator or a genuine social reformer?"

I replied that he was perhaps a bit of both but that you could not put Arabs like him into conveniently docketed slots.

"Well, we don't like him much for what he says about us," came the retort, "but he must be a lot better than Hussein."

I expressed surprise.

"It's simple," said the young Englishman. "Nasser says he's going to have an election but Hussein, having had one and got an answer from it that he didn't like, has dissolved his Parliament. That's like Hitler!"

I tried to explain the true situation, to tell them about the system of bought politicians and rigged elections in Jordan and elsewhere. But no, they could not understand. The final shock was when we turned to Syria.

"Now," said the Kibbutz leader, supported by a number of his friends, "there's something far better than Jordan. The Syrians had an election the other day and the left wing won."

I gave up. These young, courageous patriotic pioneers being mostly of a left-wing persuasion themselves, just could not understand the fallacy, in the Middle East especially, of the old saying that Left can speak to Left. They firmly believed that a left-wing Arab was full of understanding for left-wing Israel and

that the only thing preventing him from getting together with
his political associates across the border was the system of re-
actionary kings and right-wing governments. Get rid of Hussein
and Nuri and put socialist governments in their place and all
would be well between Israel and the Arabs.

We may say that this is only the ignorance of youth. But
youth is Israel and Israel is the young men and women in the
Kibbutz on the Gaza border and in the Kibbutzes everywhere
else. The ignorance I saw is the ignorance of Israel, of a nation
of people blinded by their own bravery, who know nothing of
the principal problem which stands between them and a state
of peace—the fears and suspicion of the Arab world.

Ben Gurion alone of the political leaders I met seemed able
to understand anything of the Arab mentality. He confessed a
great admiration for Bourguiba as a man of culture and breadth
of view and he seemed to pin some hopes on the Tunisian Prime
Minister as a potential educator of Arab opinion. But, unlike
the majority of his leading advisers, Ben Gurion is an old
Palestinian, who has lived amongst the Arab world since the
beginning of this century. His Foreign Ministry is led by a
lady who came to Israel from Milwaukee after the Second
World War and most of its top officials are equally recent
arrivals.

I spent a long time with Mrs Meier, the Foreign Minister,
discussing every aspect of Israeli foreign policy. I had been told
that I would find her a mere echo of Ben Gurion with no particular mind of her own. What I found was a mind far more
rigid than Ben Gurion's. I might almost say, a mind closed to
any thought or suggestion which might help to reduce the
tension in Arab-Israel relations or to make things easier for
more moderate Arab counsels to prevail over the extremists.
We talked about the Suez Canal and the Gulf of Aqaba. Israel
would assert her right of passage by force at least through
Aqaba, was Mrs Meier's attitude from first to last. Useless to
point out that this blustering attitude only helped Nasser by
forcing his Arab brethren to speak up in support of his blockade.
Useless too to suggest that Israel would gain far more credit
internationally by submitting her case to the International
Court than by trying to shoot her way through Suez. Mrs Meier
held that Israel had exhausted the U.N. procedures by going

to the Security Council in 1951. It was now up to the Security Council to see that their resolution, which upheld Israeli rights, was honoured. If they did not, Israel would know what sort of friends she had in the United Nations.

Mrs Meier went on to say that whether they succeeded in forcing the Suez blockade or not, the Israelis intended to go ahead with their plans to build an oil pipe line from the Gulf of Aqaba to the Mediterranean to reactivate the Haifa refinery and put Israel back on the map of refined oil sellers. By crossing only Israeli territory this project would by-pass the Canal and, if there were any trouble with the Arabs over Aqaba, Israeli escorts would take the tankers through by force.

I endeavoured to point out that, although the Arabs might turn a blind eye to an occasional tanker going to Elath with enough oil to light the lamps of Israel, they would be sure to react violently if this traffic were stepped up to feed a pipe line which was intended to by-pass the Suez blockade. Moreover, that was not the only card in the Arab hand, as I had been reminded in places like Baghdad. They could stop the flow of oil at source. As things are today, Iranian oil is going to Elath at the rate of one tankerful per month. The National Iranian Oil Company have officially forbidden even this amount in deference to Arab requests. But the consignments are handled by a subsidiary company and being of insignificant quantities no obstacle is put in their way, either at source or in the Gulf of Aqaba. But any substantial increase would be bound to call a halt to the whole business. The Iranians would never allow it to leave or, if they did, the Arabs would never allow it to arrive.

Mrs Meier brushed all these arguments aside. Israel had a right to buy oil and Egypt had no right to prevent her. If the Iranians played the Egyptian game, then again Israel would know who were her friends and who were not.

This continuous harping on the theme of testing out her friends—a theme which I had heard from many of Mrs Meier's compatriots during my visit and also in my Foreign Office days beforehand—suggests all too clearly that, like some of her Arab neighbours, Israel prefers a grievance to a reconciliation. A grievance helps to unite the people and to bring home to benefactors overseas the need to go on being beneficent. A reconciliation policy would cause major internal convulsions and might even lead to a drying up of outside aid.

I certainly found Israeli grievances working overtime about the U.N. and its Emergency Force. Mr Hammarskjöld was only a little less unpopular than Colonel Nasser for his alleged discrimination against Israel and softness towards Egypt. The U.N. Emergency Force was under heavy fire for being subservient to the Egyptian Army Command. There was no Israeli prepared to give it any credit for the almost complete peace and quiet which reigned on Israel's borders after the U.N. took up its stand.

This bitterness and contempt for the U.N. is tragic and unwise. In the first place the Emergency Force could have been the beginnings of something very great, had Israel been ready to accept its presence on her side of the frontier. Not only could it have become a physical barrier against all attacks from either side; it might too have set the precept for a really effective international police force. Apart from this, it helps no one who wants to see a settlement for Israeli spokesmen to sow constant distrust of the U.N. amongst their own people. As M. Ardalan, Iran's Foreign Minister, told me, only the United Nations could resolve the Arab-Israel conflict. That is true, though the day when they can go to work is still distant, perhaps even more distant as a result of the Suez tragedy. However much those countries may complain about the U.N. who have found themselves in conflict with it or have felt that it has not always secured a fair settlement of their disputes, the fact remains that the vast majority of nations believe in it and look to it for justice and protection. No other body and no other group of nations has the same title of impartiality with the Arab States to take on the task of squaring that vicious circle—the Palestine dispute.

But the day when the U.N. can go to work on this perplexing problem with any hope of success is still distant, and the Suez tragedy certainly brought it no nearer. Even though Israel will now probably stay within her borders, there can be no settlement while mass immigration continues and while the Arabs feel militarily weaker and economically inferior to Israel. It will take the Arabs a long time to achieve even technological equality. Iraq has made a good start and has given a lead; but only a united effort can bring success and Arab unity will take

time. As Israeli Foreign Ministry chiefs made clear to me, Israel
will use every device to keep her Arab neighbours divided. The
Fertile Crescent to them wears an offensive, not a defensive,
look; Arab unity means to Israel, not a posture of equality from
which to negotiate, but an eminence from which to dictate
terms or to launch an avenging war.

Meanwhile there is one problem which cannot await a
general settlement—the Arab refugees. If nowhere else this
ever-growing Communist infection must be tackled in Jordan,
where they number 600,000. Four governments hold the key—
America, Britain, Jordan and Israel. If Israel would take back
100,000 or so America and Britain should spare neither money
nor effort to get Jordan to resettle the residue by promoting
large-scale irrigation schemes.

I discussed this with Ben Gurion, pointing out the continuing
danger to Israel of these homeless, hopeless thousands sitting
and multiplying on her very doorstep. Israel could not rule out
the chance that one day they might decide to walk in a body
back into Israel and take over their land. What could the
Israelis do to stop them? Shoot them? Or try to push them
back? It was clear that Ben Gurion did not relish the prospect.
Speaking very solemnly, he said that if Jordan played her part
as well Israel would help to resettle in Israel a number—he
would not venture an exact figure—of the Arab refugees now
in Jordan. "Even without a general settlement?" I asked, and
Ben Gurion nodded his assent. But he was quick to add that if
Jordan failed to honour her side of the bargain, the deal would
be off.

True such a scheme does not meet the claim for full restitu-
tion of Arab rights. But security, let alone prosperity, make it
imperative for Jordan to settle for half a loaf. Also if Israel can
figuratively settle another 2,000,000 Jews that she is unlikely
to collect, she can presumably resettle 100,000 Arab refugees.
Ben Gurion certainly did not contest this.

Such a project would be admittedly only a partial settlement.
But the cancer of the refugee problem requires urgent surgery.
Who can say that the operation might not be a first step to-
wards a general recovery of health and stability in the Middle
East? At least there can be no harm in trying.

CHAPTER XIII

EGYPT

I HAD not been to Egypt or seen Colonel Nasser for two and a half years. I was therefore prepared for some surprises when I reached Cairo at the end of my long journey. I certainly got my fill. But with the best will in the world I cannot say I found anything changed for the better. Everywhere beneath the ebullient surface of natural gaiety there was deterioration. Egypt (and Nasser) had gone downhill fast.

Cairo wore the festive façade of the Bairam holiday. The Nile was a seething, screaming mass of Egyptian youth in rowing boats working off some of the gastronomic blow-out with which they had celebrated the end of the month's fast of Ramadan. This was where I came in (or rather went out) last time. Then the same scenes and sounds had greeted the signing of the Anglo-Egyptian Treaty of 1954 by Nasser and myself. Fireworks by night, boating by day and shouting by both was still the holiday routine of these simple, child-like people.

I looked around for signs of development, but saw scarcely any. A few new blocks of flats had been completed, the fun fairs seemed to have been enlarged, and a new Shephard's Hotel had sprung up on the banks of the Nile between the Hotel Semiramis and the British Embassy, closed and empty like a gigantic vault. But the new "Shephard's" could not open because there was no tourist traffic to fill it. The Semiramis where I stayed was at most one-eighth full. I do not know whether Colonel Nasser meant things to work out that way, but he has certainly "nationalized" Egypt. Apart from diplomats, I only saw five Europeans in the time I spent in Cairo. Alexandria, I was told, was even worse. A city whose life depended on the foreigner, the foreign business houses, banks, insurance companies, and the like, Alexandria since the nationalization of these enterprises is a dead and empty place.

Nasser himself I found greatly changed from the man I negotiated with in 1954. Only his sense of humour remained the same. Gone was the hope of playing a neutral rôle between West and East, of playing one off against the other. Gone were the hopes of giving a lead towards an Arab-Israel settlement of which he had spoken with some optimism before. The beady-black and penetrating eyes had lost much of the old bravado. The bombastic arrogance with which he used even to conduct private discussions now seemed to be reserved solely for the public platform. Here confronting me was a man who knew he had taken the wrong turning but did not dare to turn back, who admitted he was far sold out—economically if not politically—to the communist bloc, who realized he was fast forfeiting the friendship of his fellow Arabs.

Throughout our talk he seemed resigned more than relaxed. "If the West will not help Egypt, I shall go with Russia," was his constant theme, reiterated in a tone of sorrow rather than anger.

Nasser affected to have been completely misunderstood by the West and especially by the Western press. As an example he cited some articles which I myself had written in the *New York Herald Tribune* earlier in the year. "You too," he said, "have shown that you are the dupe of the Western press." (When later Nasser seemed surprised that I still lived in England, say-ing that he had read in some London paper that I was moving to New York, I could not resist saying, "Mr President, I really have not been exiled yet. Can it be that you have become the dupe of the Western press?" His old sense of humour had not deserted him and he laughed heartily at the thrust.)

He also laughed heartily when I told him that in anything I had written about him I had only been judging from the plans of conquest which he had outlined in his own book, *The Philosophy of the Revolution.* "You should not write books," I said, "if you don't want people to take them seriously. There was another fellow who wrote a book similar to yours not long ago but nobody took him seriously at the time. We've learned better since."

"Oh! but those were only pipe dreams about military strategy," was his disingenuous reply.

I told him he could not get away with that. What about Egyptian pressures on the Sudan, Libya, Jordan, Syria and Saudi Arabia, not to speak of the Persian Gulf? Nasser admitted that he (or rather Major Salah Salem who was now under house arrest) had overplayed the hand in the Sudan. But he avowed he was not paying "one piastre" or using any pressure in Jordan.

When I said that no Jordanian from the King downwards believed this, he admitted he was now completely estranged from King Hussein. "But," he added like a desperate gambler disclosing his hand, "I am not estranged from the people."

Since he had studiously avoided mentioning King Saud, I asked how he felt about his former ally changing sides. His reply was to switch the conversation to Syria. Try as I might, I could not draw him on the topic of his former Saudi ally.

When I taxed him with his piratical behaviour over the Suez canal, he replied that Mr Dulles's sudden somersault over the Aswan Dam had struck him as a Western plot to pressure Egypt. He had therefore shown that small countries could make trouble for big. He did not contest my argument that nationalization had removed the international guarantees contained in the 1888 convention. But he would not admit that Egypt owed it to anyone to put them back. I reminded him that in the early autumn of 1956 Dr Fawzi had accepted a form of international financial control in negotiating with Mr Selwyn Lloyd in New York. That, he said, was "before the hostilities". Public opinion would not now accept any foreign pressure on Egypt. But he was willing to turn his declaration into an international agreement. Dr Fawzi later qualified this, saying that Egypt could not allow Israel to sign such an agreement.

As if by mutual arrangement, very little was said by either of us about the Anglo-French intervention at Suez. Like every other Arab, Nasser took the view that it was typical of the French but quite out of character for Britain to do such a thing in such a fashion. In fact, so he told me, after he had nationalized the Canal Company, he asked his intelligence departments for their estimate of the chances of Britain attacking Egypt on her own or at the side of Israel. The answer he got back was 6 to 4 against a British solo effort, no chance whatever of an Anglo-Israeli combination. When, therefore, he received the British ultimatum on October 30, 1956, ordering him to withdraw from the Canal and make room for the Anglo-French Forces to move in, he could not believe that we were serious.

His conspiratorial mind told him that this was a British ruse to keep his best forces in Port Said and thereby to allow the Israelis to overrun the Sinai peninsular and gain the east bank of the Canal. He had therefore immediately sent his crack formations into Sinai. I found this a curious admission that in fact the cream of his army had been routed by the Israelis.

No doubt Nasser did not realize fully the implication of what he was saying. But it would not be the first time that this has happened. Several times in our negotiations in 1954 he would let fall a careless remark which betrayed a weakness in his position. Nor would it have been the first time that the tortuous processes of his mind had seen a conspiracy where there was none. This explains much of the Swinburn/Zarb trial, and the constant arrests of people of no consequence at all on charges of spying and plotting against the régime. When I warned him of the very grave consequences which might follow if Swinburn, Zarb or their fellow prisoners were savagely dealt with, he claimed that in the West every man's hand was against him and he must protect himself against their conspiracies.

As to Israel, Nasser said that he had given up hope and abandoned all contacts with Israel soon after Ben Gurion had become Prime Minister and Moshe Sharett, who had been a moderating influence as Foreign Minister up till then, had been removed from office. These evil omens were borne out when a short while later, in early 1955, the Israelis had launched their devastating raid on Gaza, killing over 60 Egyptians and wounding several hundreds. This had confirmed his worst suspicions that Ben Gurion did want to destroy Egypt.

I pointed out that Ben Gurion had come to the same kind of conclusion about Nasser from the moment that he started buying arms from the Soviets. But this only led the Colonel into the familiar monologue about the arms and other help that the West had given to Israel and refused to Egypt. On this count he was particularly bitter against the United States, who, he alleged, had tried to starve Egypt into submitting to their imperialist designs and who were helping Israel by private donations as well as Government grants. He merely shrugged his shoulders when I suggested that nobody had done more than he and his ministers to create the state of tension which brought forth these gifts and grants from Israel's sympathizers abroad.

If he wanted to reduce the flow of aid to Israel he could do worse than reduce the tension which prompted it. Best of all would be to make peace. But Nasser would have none of this. On Israel he was one of the blind who would not see.

By far the most difficult truth to discover in Egypt is about the economic situation. There is still the same grinding poverty —and some discontent. It is hard to see how long commercial life can be carried on under a system of nationalization run by a group of young officers, who have become one of the largest holding companies of foreign capital in the world, and whose inexperience is hardly made up for by their enthusiasm.

Nasser told me that he intended to start in 1958 with the first phase of the High Dam. This will cost £60,000,000 spread over five years. For irrigation only, it will bring an extra 700,000 acres into 3-crop cultivation. Apart from this, all development schemes are being drastically cut, due to the Western squeeze curtailing capital imports.

Yet any immediate economic crisis is unlikely. Provided Egypt can sell her cotton crop, the fellaheen can tighten their belts and survive for some time on their pastoral economy. Of course it is here that the Communist stranglehold will make itself most felt. Nasser admitted that his cotton crop was mortgaged to the Soviet bloc—principally China, Russia and Poland—who were buying it in one-third instalments. A splendidly exploitable position for Soviet blackmail.

Politically I would not expect any sudden changes either. Nasser has kept the evidence of his crumbling empire from his own people, and his prestige victory over Suez will last him for quite a while. True, as one Western diplomat put it, Nasser is the leader of a revulsion and not a revolution. He has got rid of an old corrupt system without putting any effective government in its place. But equally, with one of the most nosy and efficient secret police services in the world serving the régime, there is at present no one to take his place. Nor will there be, until Egypt's exposure to Russian blackmail, having estranged the whole Arab world outside, has aroused a sufficient panic reaction within to throw up a government prepared to do serious business with the West.

Western policy should therefore be to let Nasser go on over-playing his hand and isolating himself. With the basic economic stability of a pastoral State and with no immediate political alternative, he may take longer than Mossadeq to hang himself. Though they cannot in the long run save him, the Canal revenues may help prolong his tenure. Whilst lack of Saudi cash has reduced his powers of mischief making, he can, like a wounded beast at bay, still lash out at nearby weaker brethren; and Libya, Jordan, and Kuwait are well within his range.

But Nasser, as all his actions have shown, is a conspirator, not a statesman. In this rôle he has offended and estranged his friends and braced and forewarned his enemies. This, plus his flirtation with Moscow, is losing him the campaign to subject the Arab world to his dominion; and, as he revealed very clearly to me, he knows it. Provided the West do not ruin everything by attacking or assisting him, he will in due course meet a conspirator's fate.

CHAPTER XIV

CONCLUSION

How should I sum up the impressions I formed upon this long and fascinating journey? I confess that I set out fearing the worst. I returned relieved by much of what I had seen and found, convinced that our friends are stronger and our enemies are weaker than in the critical concluding months of 1956.

In the battle that is now joined we have a host of friends in the so-called "neutral" countries, such as Morocco, Tunisia, Lebanon, Jordan and Saudi Arabia, as well as of course in the committed countries of the Baghdad Pact—Iraq, Turkey, Iran and Pakistan. Though these friends took a terrible beating over Suez, their trust in the West remains. We can still help them to win if we play our part with sincerity, loyalty and sympathy.

Of course there are still some question marks and danger spots—in Algeria, Kuwait, Bahrain, Libya and even Iran. Nasser or Communism, or both, could still make the same mess of these places that they have made of Syria and Jordan. The present favourable balance of opinion is by no means indestructible. Communism has gone deep in a few places. This is where it has been able to link backward social conditions with foreign exploitation or, taking a leaf out of Hitler's book and allying itself with Arab nationalism, to exploit the Zionist sore as did Nazi Germany in its day.

It is impossible to exaggerate the bitterness of Arab feeling on the Israeli issue. Like the sand in the desert, it gets into everything. This is not a matter of anti-Jewish sentiment. Throughout the Arab and Ottoman Empires, Jews often found toleration and refuge under Moslem rule from European persecution. But to the Arab the Israeli State means dispossession of his lands and displacement of his brothers in betrayal of the pledges of Arab unity and independence given by Britain to gain Arab support in World War I. Bad enough that after the war Britain should have carved up the Arab world into separate Kingdoms and Protectorates and shared the spoils with France. But to set up under the Balfour Declaration first a national Jewish home and then a separate Israeli State came as a deliberate assault on the Arab homeland. This wound will heal only very slowly. The Suez tragedy not only reopened it, but poured a bucketful of salt into the raw and tender flesh.

It is futile in this climate of injured opinion to suggest peace by a compromise over frontiers or refugees. The Arab will not as yet contemplate a settlement. He is still suffering from a paradoxical conflict of hope and fear—hope that, through the blockade and the progressive efflux of the European Jewish elements back to Europe, Israel will eventually disintegrate; fear of unlimited Jewish immigration leading to unlimited Israeli expansion, economic and political, at the expense of the Arab States, who will be picked off one by one.

If the hope is not only unthinkable but presently unrealizable, the fear can only be eliminated by one development—a meaningful Arab unity. Can this be achieved? I believe it can provided the net is cast widely enough to create a unity of the Moslem world and not just a repetition of the ineffective Arab League. A young Egyptian student put it this way, "The Moslem faith is not just a creed, but a community of peoples which transcends differences of nationality. Whereas nationalism separates, Islam is a cohesive factor. When, therefore, one strives for an Arab union, one is inevitably striving for a Moslem union, for each is complementary to the other."

He is right, and the West would be well advised to relate its policy to the wider picture of the whole Moslem world and not solely to the limited negative spectacle of Egypt, Syria and Israel. Nationalism is a poor second best, with all the divisions, complexes and weaknesses it creates. But, because the rulers of the inter-war years accepted the division of the Arab world and their successors were too indolent or corrupt to try and change it, Nasser has become a popular hero whose picture adorns the bazaars from Marrakesh to Bahrain. Not only does Nasser claim to have thrown off the yoke of those who divided Arabia, but many of the inarticulate masses see in him the promise of that unity without which they cannot treat on equal terms with the West or with Israel.

But there are many also who see in Nasser a threat of

exchanging Western for Soviet imperialism. True they are mostly among the ruling classes. Nevertheless it is a significant credit item that Arabs are now warning Arabs, Moslems averting Moslems, of the Communist menace to their faith and freedom. A critically important realignment is taking place. Kings and Presidents hitherto renowned more for appeasing than for resisting Nasser are beginning to stand up to his pressures. King Saud is supporting Jordan against Egypt, and King Hussein is showing fight. Lebanon and Saudi Arabia are coming together with the Baghdad Pact powers in face of the Soviet-Syrian-Egyptian threat. Activity is stirring away from Cairo. Nasser no longer holds the only Middle-Eastern Court. It is Egypt and no longer Iraq which is becoming isolated.

Yet it will need more than the comings and goings of rulers to cement an Islamic Alliance. Above all it will need an economic foundation. The economic pressures are beginning to assert themselves. The problems of oil revenues and inflation, of the haves and the have-nots, the division of revenues from pipe lines, and the need to find markets for the products of new industries, are all creating the need for economic integration. To give one example, Iraq could produce all the cement for the Middle East if the markets were open to her.

It is not surprising, therefore, that in those countries such as Iraq which are ready to act rather than just talk about unity, the European Common Market has attracted much interest. Some such scheme might well form the basis of a developing Moslem Confederation.

It is here that the Eisenhower Doctrine and Anglo-American aid to the Baghdad Pact can play their most effective part, by promoting joint development projects and by under-pinning the economies of the weaker brethren.

Despite the siren voices of the Soviets, the Arab world still looks to the West for help and guidance. American influence and credit is considerable, and so still is British—though it took a hard knock over Suez. Above all things the Arabs want our trade, and they trust and respect our traders.

India and Pakistan too have a considerable potential influence upon the Middle East. Pakistan is using hers; India is not. President Mirza told me he could do more to help, especially in the Persian Gulf. But when he suggested before his recent visit to King Saud that he might help over Buraimi, he had been bluntly told by London to lay off.

This is short-sighted policy, the more so since India looks East not West—in several hours of discussion Pandit Nehru talked almost exclusively to me of Russia and China. India's attitude to the Middle East is negative. Nehru prefers that nationalism not internationalism should be the watchword of the Moslem world. He does not want Islamic union. He wants Pakistan to be isolated—hence his hostility to the American Aid Programme and to the alliances of which Pakistan is a member, such as the Baghdad Pact. Most of all Nehru wants to be the arbiter of Asia and an alliance of 300 million Moslems would seriously challenge his claim to the title. It could also prove an irresisitible magnet to the Moslem majority of Kashmir.

Thus the struggle for power presents itself in the Middle East. Russia follows the familiar pattern of divide, exploit and subvert, allying herself with Nasser and nationalism for her purpose. India, perhaps not altogether unconsciously, aids and abets this aim. But the Islamic world is beginning to come alive to the dangers of these divisive practices. If the West, and especially Britain, can redeem its pledges and help the Moslem world to regain its unity and cohesion, we shall not only have established an unbroken line of resistance to Communism from Casablanca to Karachi; we shall have gained the friendship and esteem of one of the greatest powers in world politics for generations to come—the reawakening strength of united Islam; and we shall have helped to fulfil the essential condition whereby Arab and Jew may live in peace and the West may trade in security.